The Heinle & Heinle
ENGLISH FOR ACADEMIC PURPOSES SERIES

Series Editors

JERRY L. MESSEC
CHARLES H. BLATCHFORD

EAP ENGLISH FOR ACADEMIC PURPOSES SERIES

A Student's Guide to Handwriting

Patricia Byrd

HH Heinle & Heinle Publishers, Inc.
Boston, Massachusetts 02210, U.S.A.

Production Manager: Erek Smith
Editor-in-Chief: Stan Galek
Developmental Editor: Jean N. Dale
Production Editor: Priscilla G. Ryan

Cover and Text Design: Carol H. Rose
Chapter Opener Graphics: Rafael Millán
Handwriting: Sarah P. Grover

The author would like to thank the following people and organizations for permission to use their work: p. 3, Picture Collection, The Branch Libraries, The New York Public Library; p. 49-50, TOEFL 1983-1984 Bulletin of Information and Application Form; p. 51, Student Identification Form for Michigan Test, Testing Program, English Language Institute, University of Michigan; p. 101, Mariquitas Plantain Chips Package, National Foods Industries, Inc.; p. 112-113, *Our Physical Environment,* E. C. Pirkle, ed. 1980, Burgess Publishing Co., Minneapolis, Minnesota; Chapter 12 Handwriting, Anne Campbell, Joyce Durand, Pat Tucker, Liz Zorilo, Charlotte Stokes, Dan Dropko, Kathy Still, Sandra Fradd, and Mary Ellen Muñoz.

Heinle & Heinle Publishers, Inc.
286 Congress St
Boston, MA 02210
U.S.A.

Copyright © 1985 by Heinle & Heinle Publishers, Inc. under the Universal copyright Convention, International Copyright and Pan-American Copyright Convention.

All rights reserved. No part of this publication may be reproduced or transmitted in any form or by any means, electronic or mechanical, including photocopy, recording or any information storage and retrieval system, without permission in writing from the publisher. Manufactured in the United States of America.

ISBN 0-8384-1301-3

10 9 8 7 6 5 4 3 2 1

PREFACE

Write On: A Student's Guide to Handwriting, addresses the needs of Intermediate and higher-level students who are already familiar with English and its writing system. The objective is to give students advanced skills in producing the types of handwriting most commonly used in American colleges and universities. While developing this skill, the student learns to read and understand individual variations in standard handwriting styles. Exercises are geared toward Academic experiences such as note-taking, filling out forms, and reading and duplicating blackboard assignments.

The text can be used in conjunction with English composition courses or for academic skills preparation, as handwriting practice can be added to an ESL/EFL curriculum without disturbing the program's basic structure. Students may work independently, as would occur in individualized lab work, or in small groups with occasional supervision. They could also do the exercises as homework assignments. It is important to note that to avoid tiring, it is best to work at penmanship for only 15-20 minutes at a time.

Practice sequences in this text can easily be assigned as a flexible activity in a writing or multi-skills course, and motivated students will find its utilitarian approach extremely helpful in the mastery of both printing and cursive styles of writing. Explanations are thorough and the student is given plenty of opportunity for practice. Readings interspersed throughout the text cover such topics as the origin of certain letters, Chinese characters, and the variety of alphabet styles that exist around the world. Basic to the purpose of this text, students are treated as intelligent, academically oriented adults, who have taken this opportunity to improve their English handwriting skills.

ACKNOWLEDGMENT

In addition to giving a sample of his unique handwriting, Jerry Messec has given editorial advice that has greatly improved this text. His enthusiasm for the project has made the writing of the explanations and the exercises an interesting intellectual as well as pedagogical experience.

INTRODUCTION

Printed and cursive styles of handwriting are both used in the United States today. This derives from the nature of our educational system, which teaches writing in two separate stages. Students first learn to write a very plain style, commonly called "printing", "block writing", or more professionally, "manuscript." Here are some examples of this first style:

The chemical symbol for water is H_2O.
The earth revolves around the sun.

Two major characteristics distinguish **printing** from other forms of writing:

- No connections are made between letters.
- Letters are made with straight lines, circles, or part-circles.

The second stage of handwriting instruction in the United States teaches students to write a style called "cursive" or script." Here are the same two sentences written in **cursive**:

The chemical symbol for water is H_2O.
The earth revolves around the sun.

Unlike printing, cursive is distinguished by its use of:

- Slanted letters (leaning slightly to the right)
- Connecting lines
- Curved lines and loops

In theory, printing is merely a temporary tool of early childhood education; in reality this is not the case. Some people prefer to print because they like the neat, clean, simple style of printing. Many people develop a mixed style in which they connect small letters with print-style capitals, connect some letters while leaving a separation between others, or use some letters of one shape and some of another. Chapter 12 has many examples.

Printing has become a necessary skill for students at all levels of education in the United States. There are two important reasons:

1. Printing is required on many common forms, papers, and documents of every sort.
2. Being able to read the printed or mixed-cursive-and-printed handwriting of others—teachers, fellow students, clerks, secretaries, etc.—is essential.

A third style of writing, called italic, is becoming popular with some schools and teachers. Italic is a very attractive handwriting style, but since the form is not yet generally used in the United States, it will not be taught in this text.

The chemical symbol for water is H_2O.
The earth revolves around the sun.

The traditional goals of penmanship are:

- legibility
- speed
- economy of effort

Some people might add visual beauty to the list, but since our purposes here are primarily functional, we will focus on the first three goals.

Legibility in your writing will allow others to be able to read it accurately and easily. This is very important for a student. When a teacher has trouble reading handwriting, the student tends to get lower grades. Obviously, it is also important to be able to write class notes accurately and quickly, making sure they are legible for further study.

The following all contribute to legibility:

- correct formation of the shape of letters
- correct spacing
- correct size of letters
- correct slant (for cursive)
- correct placement of lettering (on lines)
- use of a conventional style of letters

Speed of writing varies from context to context. Legibility tends to decrease as writing speed increases. When printing an application form, the applicant is generally not in a hurry. But when taking notes during a lecture, there is not time enough to make each letter perfectly. It is important to practice maintaining legibility while regularly increasing writing speed.

When first learning a physical skill like handwriting, more energy is needed to perform the task correctly. There is little **economy of effort**. The eye and hand muscles are learning to do new things which require a high level of coordination. Be patient. If you practice with effort and attention you will dramatically improve your handwriting.

CALLIGRAPHIC CHAPTER OPENERS

Chapter 1 Specimen of the Magna Charta, engraved from one of the original copies
p. 3   in the British Museum. Courtesy New York Public Library Picture
          Collection.
          Copy of the Seal of King John. Courtesy New York Public Library
          Picture Collection.

Chapter 2 Arthur Baker: *Brush Calligraphy*. New York: Dover Publications, Inc.,
p. 11   1984

Chapter 3 Cervantes: *Don Quixote de la Mancha* in Hindustani translation (Calcutta,
p. 19   1903) and Russian translation (Moscow, 1815).

Chapter 4 Protestant hymn published in Prague in 1566.
p.27

Chapter 5 Characters:
p. 33   1. Ethiopian
           2. Persian arrow-headed
           3. Magadha (older Sanscrit)
           4. Sanscrit
           5. Ancient greek
           6. Zeud
           7. Chinese

Chapter 6 Initial verses of *Argonautica (The Quest of Jason for the Golden Fleece)*,
p. 45   written by Apollonius of Rhodes in the Third Century B.C.

Chapter 7 *Chronica del . . . . Principe y Rey don Alfonso el Onzeus. . .* Valladolid
p. 63   (Spain), 1551.

Chapter 8 Carolingian documentary cursive; 10th century. Arthur Blake: *Historic
p. 73   Calligraphic Alphabets*. New York: Dover Publications, Inc., 1980.

Chapter 9 Translation by Majid Fakhry in "Lincoln's Gettysburg Address in
p. 79   Translation" compiled by Roy P. Basler, Published by Library of
           Congress, 1972, ISBN 0-8444-0018-1

Chapter 10 Leonardo da Vinci (1452-1519)
p. 91   Johann Sebastian Bach (1685-1750)
            Johann Wolfgang von Goethe (1749-1832)
                Domenico Theotocopůli, "El Greco" (1541-1614)
            Amerigo Vespucci (1454-1512)
                Diego R. de Silva y Velásques (1599-1660)
            Mao Tse-Tung (1893-1976)
                Blaise Pascal (1623-1662)

Chapter 11 Beijin
p. 103   Shanghai
            Guangzhou
            Dairen = Liaoning
            Wuhan

Chapter 12 Page of Boccaccio's codex on Dante's life (Toledo).
p. 117

CONTENTS

Preface   v
Introduction   vi
Handwriting Charts   xi
    Handwriting Is Not Just Child's Play   xiv

PART ONE: Printing   1

CHAPTER ONE   Capital Letters   4
   The Origin of Letters A, B, and C.   10
CHAPTER TWO   Lower Case Letters   12
   A Historical Note on "Lower Case" and "Upper Case"   18
CHAPTER THREE   Writing Numbers and Numerals   20
   Leonardo of Pisa   26
CHAPTER FOUR   Punctuation   28
   The World's Writing Systems   32
CHAPTER FIVE   Practice with Printing   34
   Alphabetical Writing Systems   44
CHAPTER SIX   Printing in Actual Use   46
   Analyzing and Judging Your Writing   59
   Paper Money from Around the World   60

PART TWO: Cursive   61

CHAPTER SEVEN   Capital Letters   64

The Origin and Forms of Q   71

CHAPTER EIGHT   Lower Case Letters   74

The Chinese Writing System   77

CHAPTER NINE   Combining Letters to Make Words   80

The Origin of Letters X, Y, and Z   89

CHAPTER TEN   Practice with Cursive in Sentences   92

Writing and Commerce   101

CHAPTER ELEVEN   Cursive in Actual Use   104

When Should You Type   116

CHAPTER TWELVE   Reading American Handwriting   118

Calligraphy—the Art of Writing   125

Answer Key   126
Practice Sheets   128

PRINTING

Capital Letters

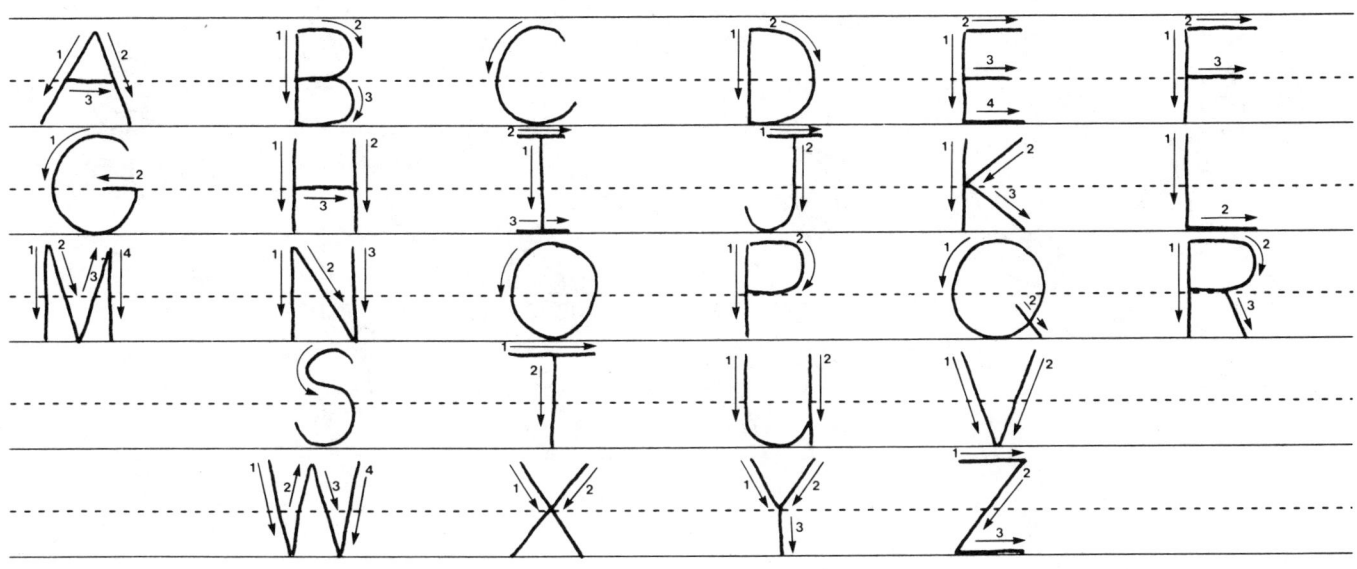

Lower Case Letters

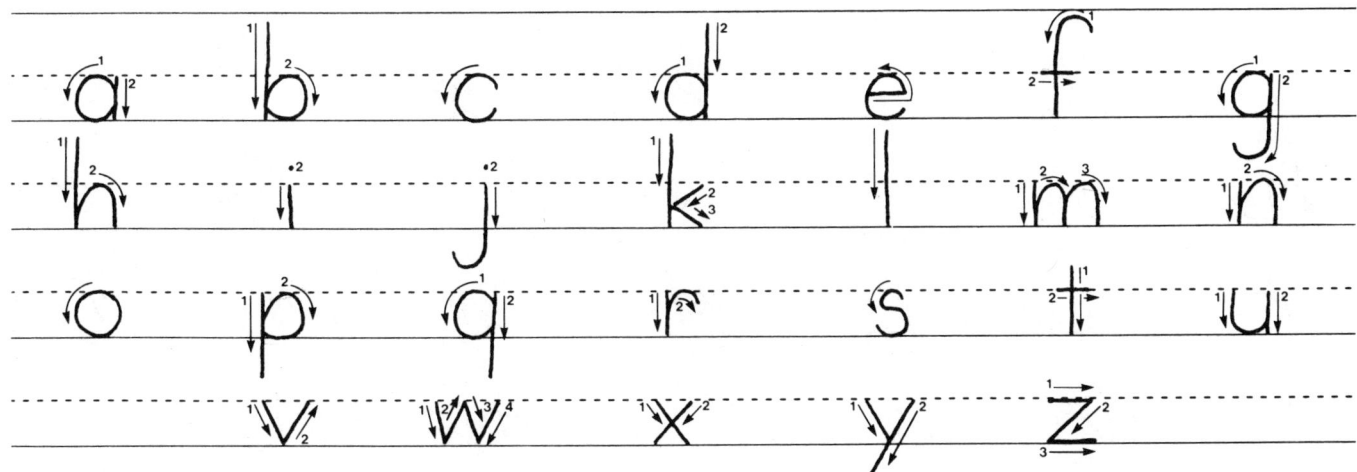

Arabic Numerals

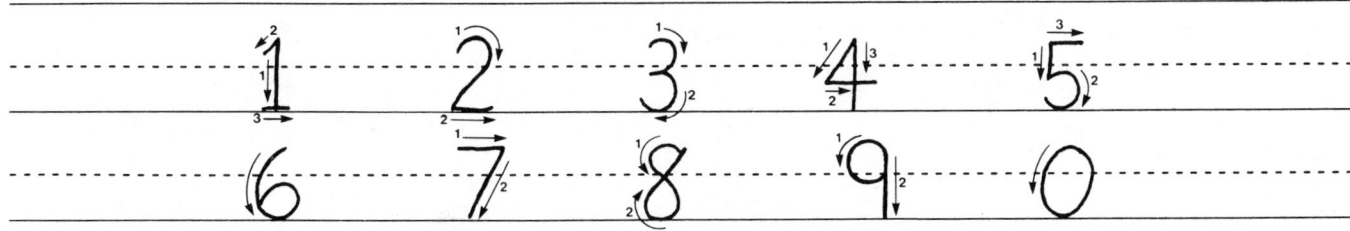

CURSIVE

Capital Letters

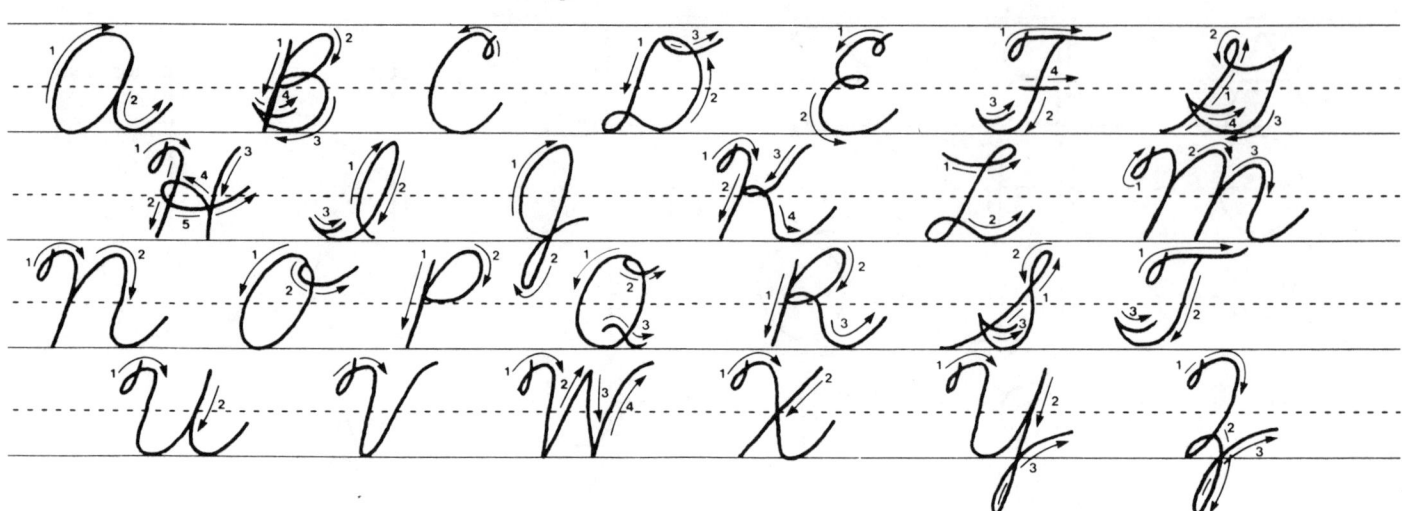

Lower Case Letters

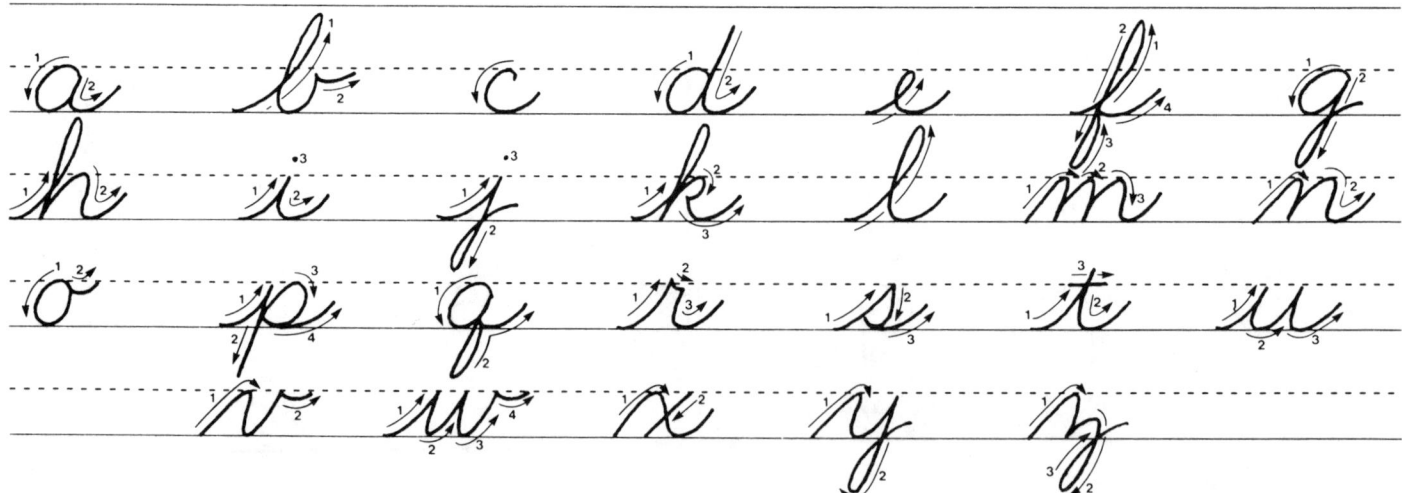

Handwriting Is Not Just Child's Play

When adults try to improve a skill like handwriting, the first emotion they feel may well be embarrassment. Perhaps thoughts like these may cross their minds: "This is what children do!" "How awkward-looking (ugly) my letters are!" This is a very natural reaction, but don't let it prevent you from gaining this important skill. One value of this text is that it can be used for self-study. This means that you can do the work privately, either at home or elsewhere. Be assured that you will gain improved handwriting skills very quickly if you practice *seriously*.

PART ONE

PRINTING

Johannes dei gra Rex Angl. Dns Hybn. Dux Normann. Aqmt. Comes Andeg. Archiepis lpis. Abbibz. Comitibz. Baronibz. Justic. Forest. vic comitibz. Prepositis. Minibs. 7 omnibz Ballivis 7 fidelibz suis Salt. — Nullus liber homo capiat ut imprionet. aut disseisiet. aut utlaget. aut exulet. aut aliquo modo destruat. nec sup eum ibimul nec sup eum mittemul nisi p legale iudicium parium suoy. ut p legem terre. — Data p manum nram in prato qd uocat Runingmed Inter Windelesoy 7 Stanes. Quto decimo die Jun. Anno Regni nostri Septimo decimo.

Printing

CHAPTER ONE

Capital Letters

Below, you see two charts of the printed letters of the Roman alphabet. Use these as models as you proceed to practice your handwriting.

Capital and Lower Case Letters

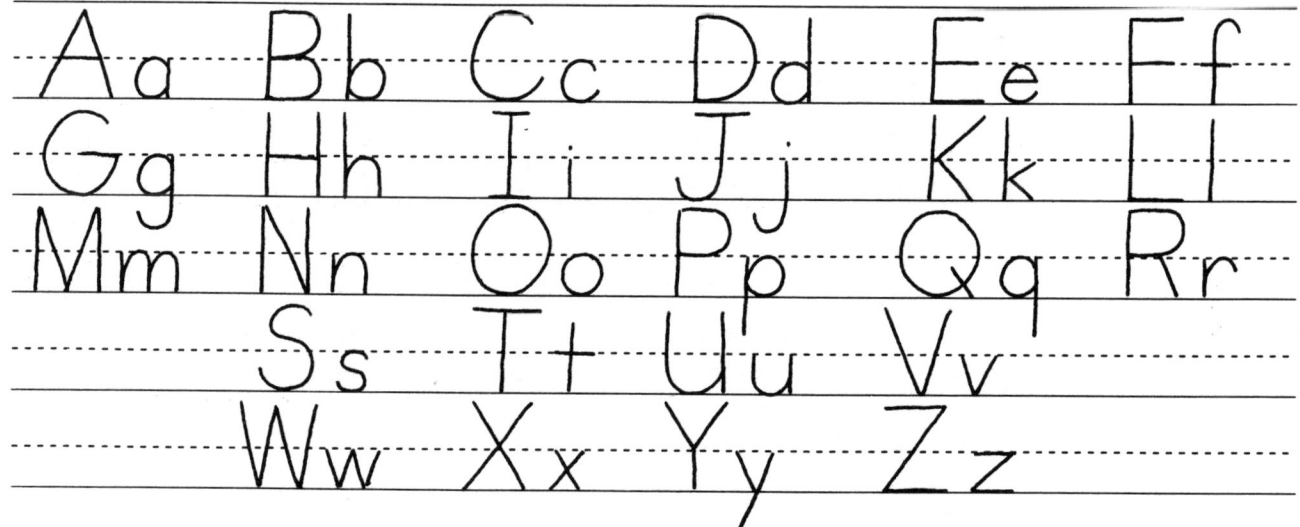

Capital Letters

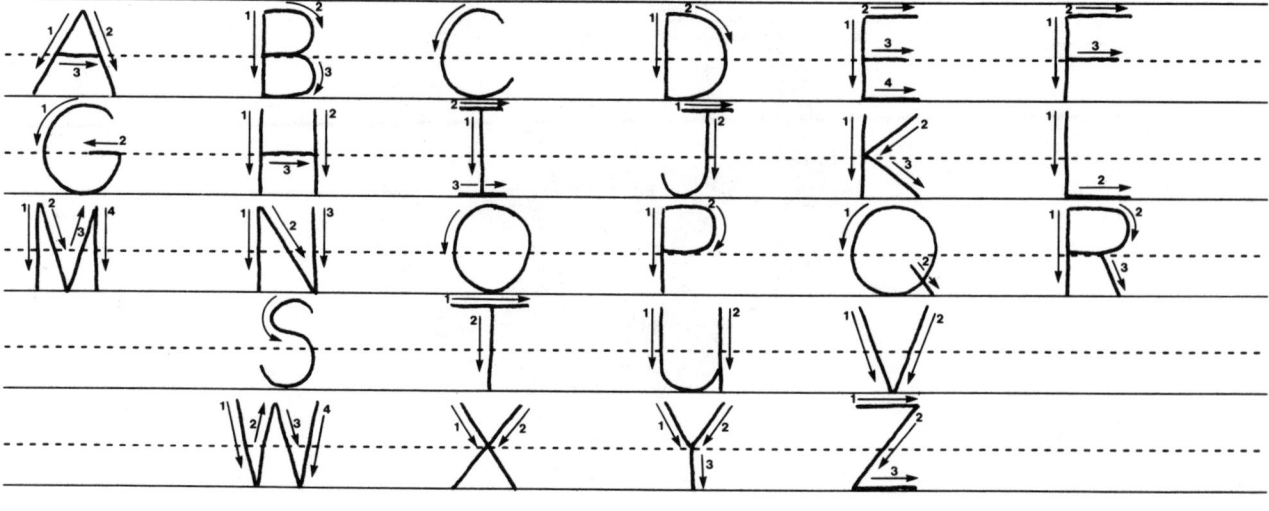

A. Forms of Printed Letters

Study each of the letters carefully. See if you can distinguish the different formations of the various letters. Below, in the blanks to the left of each letter, place an × if the letter is made with straight lines, an ○ if it is made with circles or parts of circles, or an ⊗ if it is made with a circle or part-circle combined with straight lines.

___ A	___ N	___ a	___ n
___ B	___ O	___ b	___ o
○ C	___ P	○ c	___ p
⊗ D	___ Q	___ d	___ q
___ E	___ R	___ e	___ r
___ F	___ S	___ f	___ s
___ G	___ T	___ g	___ t
× H	___ U	⊗ h	___ u
___ I	___ V	___ i	___ v
___ J	___ W	___ j	___ w
___ K	___ X	___ k	___ x
___ L	___ Y	___ l	___ y
___ M	___ Z	___ m	___ z

We do not use capital letters to form whole words very often, but there are a few exceptions. For example, we use them when labeling file folders, when writing titles of handwritten papers, and in writing address labels.

RECORDS FOR CAR

We frequently see capitals used without lower case letters in signs and printed materials for the purpose of catching our attention.

We are taught to imagine a second line running between the printed lines.

Capital letters fill almost the entire space. Lower case letters fit the bottom half of the space (although there are exceptions as you can see). The dotted line represents the middle of a capital letter. Lower case letters are approximately half the size of capital letters.

The exercises that follow will give you practice in the correct formation of capital letters. While practicing, be sure to:

- Fill the line using the letter at left as a model.
- Make a well-formed letter and place the letter correctly on the line.
- Form the letters by following the lines in the order of the numbered arrows.
- Start all letters at the top.
- Notice that letters are usually formed by writing from left to right. (For example, in making an **E**, you make a long straight line on the left and then three short lines, moving from top to bottom and from left to right.)
- Make letters the same size as the model.
- Place the paper straight in front of you or only slightly angled to the left as shown below.

- Place the paper straight in front of you or only slightly angled to the left as shown below.

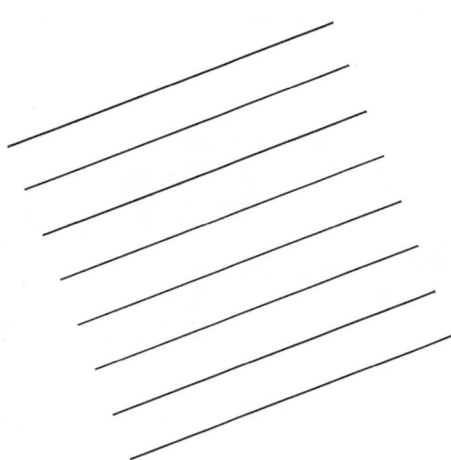

B. Straight Line Letters

Fill the line using the printed capital letter at left as a model.

E
F
H
I
L
T
A
K
M
N
V
W
X

Y
Z

C. Curved Line Letters

Fill each line with curved line capital letters.

O
C
S

D. Straight and Curved Line Letters

These letters combine curves with straight lines. Fill each line with examples of these mixed-shape letters.

D
G
Q
J
U

Notice that **P**, **B**, and **R** are very much alike. **P** is a straight line with a part-circle at the top. **B** adds another part-circle of the same size at the bottom. **R** is a **P** with a slanted line added at the bottom. Practice these.

P
B
R

E. The Alphabet

1. Write the alphabet from A to Z using all capital letters.

2. Now write the alphabet from Z to A using all capital letters.

F. Alternating Letters

Practice alternating between curved and straight-line letters. Fill each line with the alternating letters:

OX
AB
CE
FG
JK
ST
TS
UV
UW

G. Names

1. Write your name using all capital letters.

2. Write the name of your country using all capital letters.

3. Write the name of the school where you are studying.

The Origin of Letters A, B, and C

The Roman (or Latin) alphabet's history started with a writing system developed by the Semitic languages of the Middle East. One version was passed to the Greeks by the Phoenicians. The Greeks modified the system by developing symbols for vowels.

The first letter of the Phoenician system was a letter that looked something like this: ∀. (It stood for a way of pronouncing a consonant.) The Greeks stood the letter up: A or A and used it to represent a vowel sound. Thus began the centuries-long process that has led to our modern shapes: A a and *Aa*.

The original Phoenician shape was named *aleph* or **ox**. Scholars think the shape had originally represented the head of an ox.

The second letter of the Latin alphabet was called *beta* by the Greeks. However, in the Semitic languages it was called *beth* or "house" because its square shape looked like the floor plan of a simple two-room house.

C started its life as an angular shape ⅄ and was called *gimel*. Some scholars think it had developed from a very early sign for "camel."

The history of these three letters shows that people have been learning from each other from the very earliest times. We are reminded that the Middle East was indeed the "cradle" of Western Civilization.

(*Encyclopedia Britannica* v. 4, p. 536, v. 2, p. 940, and v. 1, p. 1, (Chicago: Encyclopedia Britannica, Inc., 1969).

10

Printing

CHAPTER TWO

Lower Case Letters

Look again at the chart of printed letters.

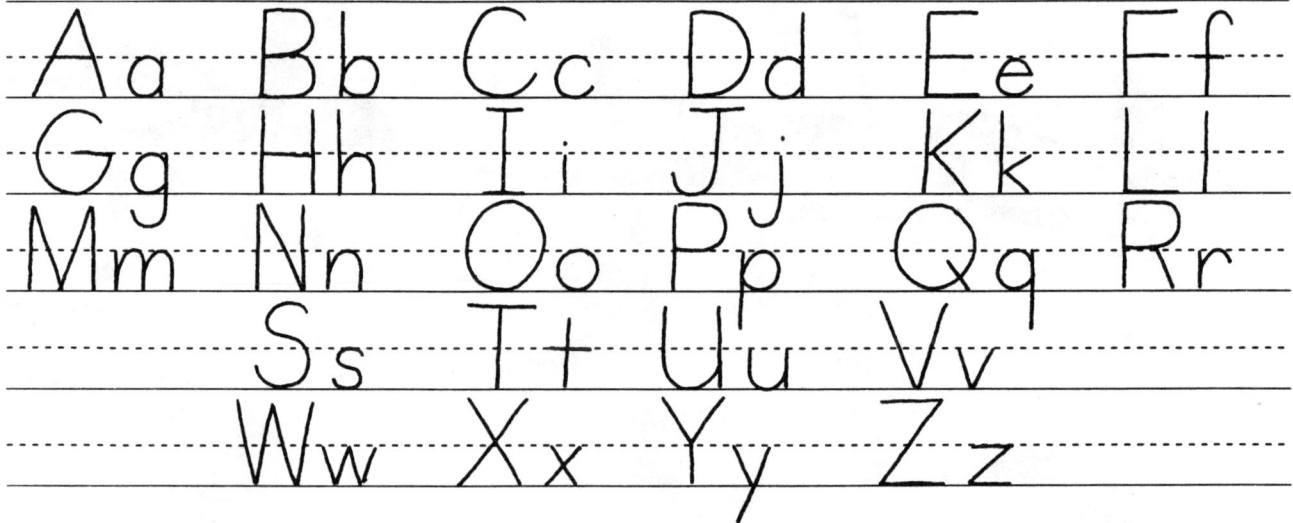

Now look at the lower case letters.

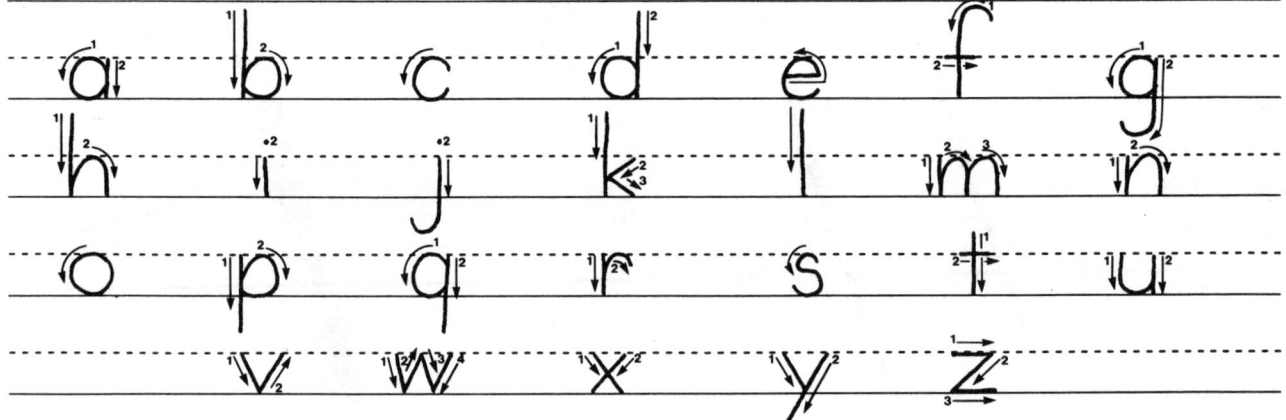

A. DIFFERENCES BETWEEN CAPITAL AND LOWER CASE LETTERS

Study the letters in the charts carefully and see if you can distinguish between the various letter formations.

1. Which letters use only straight lines? Try to print them on the line below.

   _____

2. Which use only circles with no straight lines?

   _____

3. Which use mixed lines?

   _____

Before seriously practicing these lower case letters, you need to compare them with the capital letters we have just studied. Try to explain the differences in shape by looking at the chart again.

For example, the capital **A** is made of all straight lines while the small **a** uses both part of a circle and a straight line. Of course, the capital letter is bigger than the lower case letter. Notice the difference between the typeset or typewritten **a** and the handprinted ɑ as it appears in the chart at the beginning of this chapter. Follow the style used in the chart when practicing your letters. You will find that some letters are different only in size and are shaped exactly the same—for example: Ss.

4. What other lower case letters differ from their capital letters only in size? Write them here.

   _____

B. LOWER CASE LETTERS

Practice forming these small letters making sure you place them on the line correctly. Remember that we write in the space between the two printed lines, but we imagine another line dividing that space into two sections. Most lower case letters are written between the dotted line and the bottom line, but some extend beyond the lines.

1. Which letters are written only in the space between the dotted line and the bottom line? Write them on the line.

   _____
   -
   _____

2. Which lower case letters are written beyond the dotted or solid line?

   _____
   -
   _____

C. STRAIGHT LINE LETTERS

Here are the letters which are made only with straight lines.

1. Fill the line copying the model letter.

   i
   l
   t
   v
   w
   y
   z
   k

2. Notice that **t** is not as tall as the other letters which have stems written above the dotted line. Write the letters **t** and **f** together.

   tf

D. CURVED LINE LETTERS

1. Since the **o** shape is the basis for many other letters, start by practicing making o's: Begin at the top and complete the circle by moving left and then around. This direction is the opposite of the traditional analog clock movement, so it is called "counter-clockwise." (Obviously, the traditional movement of clock hands is called "clockwise," or "the way the clock moves.")

   o

2. Now make the other two letters that use only curves.

   c
   s

E. STRAIGHT AND CURVED LINE LETTERS

These five groups of letters use both curves and straight lines.

> **Group One:** adgq
> **Group Two:** bp
> **Group Three:** e
> **Group Four:** hmn/u/r
> **Group Five:** fj

1. The letters in **Group One** are all formed by using the left half of a circle plus a straight line.

   - **a** is almost a complete circle with a straight line down the right side.
   - **d** is very like **a** but the straight line is longer.
   - To make **g** start with an **a** and add a straight line that goes down below the writing line. The line curves at the bottom.
   - **q** is different from **g** only in that the **q** does not curve at the bottom.

   Fill each line with examples of the following letters.

   a

   d

   g

   q

2. The two letters in **Group Two** use the right side of the circle to make the basic shape. Straight lines are drawn for both the **b** and the **p**. Then we add the circle.

   Fill each line with examples of the letter.

   b

   p

3. The single lower case letter **e** of **Group Three** is, as you can see, a part circle like a **c**, but intersected by a straight line. Make the straight line first (from left to right) and then add the part circle counterclockwise.

   Fill this line with **e**'s.

   e

4. The letters in **Group Four** all have a straight line on the left followed by one or more curved shapes. Notice that the curves turn into straight lines and are not circles.

   a. Fill the lines that follow the letter.

   h _____

   m _____

   n _____

   b. The **u** looks like an upside-down **n**. First make a straight line that curves at its bottom and finish by adding a straight line down the right side. Fill the lines that follow the letter.

   u _____

   c. The **r** is like an **n** with part of the right side cut off. Fill the line with **r**'s.

   r _____

5. The two letters in **Group Five** both use straight lines that have curved ends.

   - The **f** is made by starting with a curve that turns into a straight line. The line is crossed with another short straight line near its middle.
   - The **j** starts as a straight line, goes below the writing line, and then curves. It is topped with a dot like an **i**.

   Fill each line with examples of these letters.

   f _____

   j _____

F. THE ALPHABET— LOWER CASE LETTERS

1. You have practiced all of the letters in shape groups. Now review by writing the lower case letters in alphabetical order from **a** to **z**.

   _____

2. Practice writing the lower case alphabet backwards from **z** to **a**.

G. LETTER COMBINATIONS

Now practice writing these lower case letters by combining them into different pairs. Fill each line with the pair of letters given at the beginning of the line.

at
ed
ie
kn
ks
vi
qu
vo
yo
wr
xa
pn
ja
un

A Historical Note on "Lower Case" and "Upper Case"

These terms for letter size/shape differences came into use after the development of moveable type for the mechanical printing process. The metal letters were kept in trays, or cases. The big letters were up while the small letters were down. Hence, capital letters are called "upper case letters" and small letters are called "lower case letters."

Printing

CHAPTER THREE

Writing Numbers and Numerals

Chart for Arabic Numbers

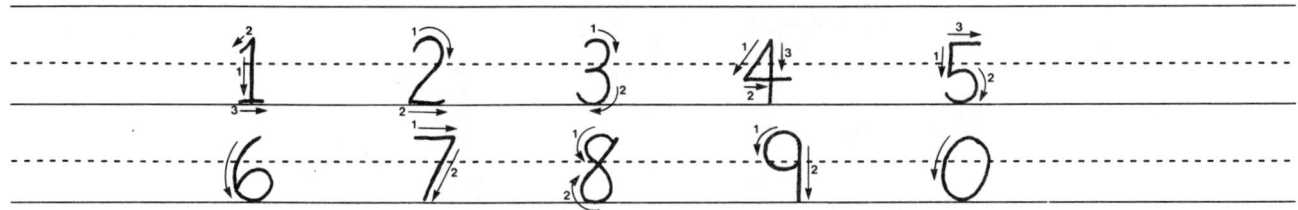

Arabic Numbers

The size of numbers may vary a little from person to person depending on the system of writing they learned as children. Numbers can be as large as capital letters or as small as lower case letters. In this text, we will write them about the height of a lower case **t**. Obviously, the size does not make that much difference so long as the shape is correct and the number is legible.

A. Problems with Arabic Numbers

Problem numbers for many people are **1**, **3**, **7**, and **5**.

1. **1** and **7** must be clearly distinguished. For this reason, some languages cross the **7**, especially those languages which make ı (one) as **1** or **1**. The crossed **7** is also used by many scientists and mathematicians in the United States. If you have this habit, you do not need to change—unless you find that you are not being understood correctly.

2. The number **3** and capital letter **E** can confuse some people especially when reading *cursive*, which you will learn later. But notice that the **3** and capital **E** are open on different sides.

3. The number **5** combines straight lines and a part-circle. It may be confused with the capital letter **S**. To avoid this, make angles at the top of this number. Be sure you make your curves *curve* and your straight lines *straight*.

4. The letter **O** is different from the number **0** (zero).

100 vs. Oklahoma or Ohio

While this is technically true (on typewriters and computers, for example), you will see that many people have one shape for both.

5. The number **6** can be confused with the lower case letter **b**. To avoid this, be sure to curve the left side of the number.

6. There are frequently used variations of some numbers:

one	l	1	1
four	4	4	4
seven	7	7	7

7. Practice writing these numbers on the lines below, making sure not to confuse them with the letters described above.

Straight lines:	1	4	7	
Curves:	3	6	8	
Combinations:	2	5	9	10

B. Number Combinations

1. Fill the line with these number combinations.

   14
   17
   13

16
18
12
15
19
10
47
37
67
78
55
94
50

2. What is your telephone number?

_____

3. What is today's date? All in numerals:

_____/_____/_____

ROMAN NUMERALS

Since the number system used in English today came to Europe from India by way of the Middle East, scholars call the system "Hindu-Arabic." Most people, however, call our number system the "Arabic number system."

Another system of writing numbers has limited, though important, use in English. They are the **Roman numerals** which were developed in Rome about the 3rd century B.C. They started being replaced in Europe in the 13th century (1200-1299) by Arabic numbers.

Roman numerals have a limited use and are never used in mathematics. Some of the places where Roman numerals are used are:

- To number the pages of a book, especially the pages of the foreword or preface (The real body of the book is usually numbered with Arabic numbers)
- To number chapters of books

- For dates (in copyright information for books and movies)
- In inscriptions on monuments
- On a building to give the date when it was built
- On some clocks and watches

The most common use of Roman numerals in U.S. universities is in outlines of materials—such as outlines of research papers. When a professor assigns a book or journal outline, he will expect the outline to use Roman numerals for the major divisions.

Although the Roman system can be used for very large numbers (especially in dates as mentioned above), you really need to know only the lower numbers. After all, books seldom have hundreds of chapters. Clocks will show only 12 hours. Outlines usually have fewer than 10 sections.

COMPARISON OF THE ROMAN AND ARABIC SYSTEMS

The Roman system is different from the Arabic system in significant ways.

- The Roman system uses letters of the alphabet as numbers. **V** is used as a letter in a word like **vocal**, but it also represents the number five in **Chapter V.** In the Arabic system, the symbols for numbers are different from the symbols for letters. The symbol **5** is not used to spell out any words.
- There is no symbol for zero in Roman numerals.
- Roman numerals do not use a system of decimal places. For example, in the Arabic system the first place on the right is for 1 to 9, the second place is for ten's, the third place for 100's, etc. This sytem makes Arabic numbers very compact and easy to use for mathematical computations.

Notice that the basic units are

I = 1   X = 10   C = 100   M = 1000
V = 5   L = 50   D = 500

A. Roman Numeral Combinations

When a lower number is placed to the left of a higher number, its value is *subtracted* from the higher number. IV is 4 (5-1). When a lower number is placed to the right of a higher number, its value is *added* to the higher number. VI is 6 (5+1). Use these rules and the list above to write these common Roman numerals.

1. What is the symbol for 9? _____

2. What is the symbol for 11? _____

3. What is the symbol for 19? _____

When two or more symbols of the same value are placed together, they are added together. X is the symbol for 10. XX is the symbol for 20.

4. How would thirty be written in Roman numerals? _____

   L is 50. But 100 is not LL! Another symbol is used: C = 100. CC is 200.

5. How would 300 be written in Roman numerals? _____

Chart of Arabic and Roman Numerals

Word in English	Arabic Numeral	Roman Numeral
one	1	I
two	2	II
three	3	III
four	4	IV
five	5	V
six	6	VI
seven	7	VII
eight	8	VIII
nine	9	IX
ten	10	X
eleven	11	XI
twelve	12	XII
thirteen	13	XIII
fourteen	14	XIV
fifteen	15	XV
sixteen	16	XVI
seventeen	17	XVII
eighteen	18	XVIII
nineteen	19	XIX
twenty	20	XX
twenty-one	21	XXI
twenty-two	22	XXII
twenty-three	23	XXIII
twenty-four	24	XXIV
twenty-five	25	XXV
twenty-six	26	XXVI
twenty-seven	27	XXVII
twenty-eight	28	XXVIII
twenty-nine	29	XXIX
thirty	30	XXX
forty	40	XL
fifty	50	L
sixty	60	LX
seventy	70	LXX
eighty	80	LXXX
ninety	90	XC
one hundred	100	C
two hundred	200	CC
three hundred	300	CCC
four hundred	400	CD

Word in English	Arabic Numeral	Roman Numeral
five hundred	500	D
six hundred	600	DC
seven hundred	700	DCC
eight hundred	800	DCCC
nine hundred	900	CM
one thousand	1000	M

To show thousands, a bar can be placed above a symbol. For example, V̄ is 5,000.

B. Various Uses of Roman Numerals

1. Roman numerals are used in outlining material.
   - I. Introductory Materials
     - A. Preface
     - B. Introduction
   - II. Printing
     - A. Capital Letters
     - B. The World's Writing Systems
     - C. Lower Case Letters
     - D. Writing Numbers and Numerals
     - E. Punctuation
     - F. Practice with Printing
     - G. Printing in Actual Use
   - III. Cursive
     - A. Capital Letters
     - B. Lower Case Letters
     - C. Letter Combinations and Words in Cursive
     - D. Practice with Cursive in Sentences
     - E. Cursive in Actual Use
     - F. Reading American Handwriting
   - IV. Answer Key

2. Clocks with Roman Numerals. There is a tradition of using IIII rather than IV for 4 that is still followed by some clock and watch makers but the use if IV is more common.

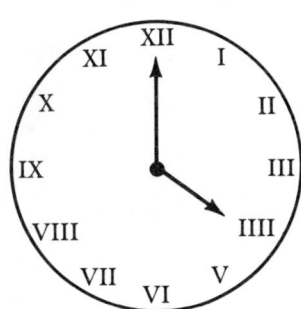

Leonardo of Pisa

At the beginning of the 13th century (1200 A.D.-1299 A.D.), merchants and scholars in Western Europe were still using Roman numerals to keep financial records and to express mathematical concepts. They used a type of abacus to do their calculations and then recorded the answers in Roman numerals. In 1202, a mathematician and merchant called Leonardo of Pisa (he was from that Italian city) or Leonardo Fibonacci (Leonardo the Son of Bonaccio) published a book called *Liber abaci* (The Book of the Abacus) in which he explained the Arabic system of numbers. He had learned the system by studying with an Arab mathematician. This book helped to popularize the Arabic system in Western Europe.

However, it took another 300 years before the Arabic system was generally understood and accepted. For a long time, people were suspicious that merchants were using the new Arabic system to hide information from them. In 1299, the government of Florence, Italy, made a law against using Arabic numbers in financial account records.

These and other interesting facts about the development of mathematics can be found in Dirk J. Struik's *A Concise History of Mathematics*, 2nd edition. New York: Dover, 1948.

Printing

CHAPTER FOUR

Punctuation

Even though we may have written all our words absolutely clearly, there is still another aspect of writing which must now be our concern, and that is **punctuation**. In order to avoid possible confusion, punctuation marks must also have the correct shape, size, and location. These examples are given for you to use for reference while you do the exercises below.

A. Period .

A period is a small dot placed on the line after the last word in a sentence.

> The earth rotates on its axis.

B. Comma ,

1. A comma looks like a period with a short tail drawn beneath it.

> The biggest export crops in the U.S. are tobacco, wheat, and corn.

2. Sometimes a comma looks like a short, slightly curved line. Many people make it perfectly straight—but it must be on the line and slanted, otherwise one might confuse it for a letter.

> ... tobacco, wheat, and corn.

In either case, the comma sits close to the word it follows. Leave a double space after the comma before starting the next word.

C. Colon :

The colon looks like two periods, one on top of the other. The colon does not rest on the line, but is slightly raised above it.

28

Chloric acid has three components: hydrogen, chlorine, and oxygen.

D. Semi-colon ;

The semi-colon is a period placed above a comma.

Benjamin Franklin was a scientist; he was also a businessman.

E. Apostrophe '

This looks like a comma placed high within a word before or after an s—above the imaginary center line.

1. What was Edison's most influential invention?

2. The scientists' cure for the disease saved many lives.

F. Quotation Marks "

These are double sets of comma-like marks. Technically, the first set is actually upside down—as in the first example. However, most people use marks like those in the second example. They are always placed high above the line before or after a word. End quotation marks generally fall outside of the other punctuation.

1. "Mathematics is the science that draws necessary conclusions." Benjamin Pierce, Linear Associative Algebra (1870) 1st sentence

2. "Mathematics is the science that draws necessary conclusions."

Note: Make sure when you are writing by hand (or typing), that you underline words that would be printed in *italics*. This means that if you ever copy a quotation that includes words printed in italic, you must underline the words that are italicized.

G. Exclamation Mark !

This is a vertical straight line over a period. In informal writing, you may use two, three or even four exclamation marks for emphasis.

> Attention! No smoking in this lab!!

H. Question Mark ?

This is a curved line over a period. The period sits on the writing line.

> What alloy of silver is used to make coins?

I. Parentheses ( )

These part-circles are used like this:

> An alloy of silver (Ag 90; Cu 10) is used to make coins.

J. Hyphen -

This is a straight horizontal mark used to connect two words or to divide a word between syllables at the end of a line.

> Modern science involves international co-operation.

> Based on prior experience, we expect this project to take two years.

K. Dash —

This is a longer mark about the size of two hyphens put together.

> Water contains only two elements—hydrogen and oxygen.

L. Brackets (or square brackets) [ ]

These are used to add information to quotations in your writing in order to make its meaning clearer. For example, if you use only one sentence from a longer passage, the pronoun reference might not be clear.

1. Look at the example below. If you wanted to use this quotation in a research paper, no one would understand who Asimov was talking about.

> "He taught himself Latin at eight and Greek at fourteen."

(Isaac Asimov, *Asimov on Numbers*. Garden City, NY: Doubleday and Co., Inc., 1977, p. 20.)

2. You cannot change Asimov's words and still use the quotation marks. But we can use brackets to add the needed information.

> "He [Gottfried Wilhelm Leibniz] taught himself Latin at eight and Greek at fourteen."

3. Brackets are also used when giving a quotation that contains an error.

> "My brother studied Portuguese in Brazill [sic]."

The word *sic* is Latin for "thus." It means "I found this exact spelling/meaning in the original."

> "Everyone knows that two plus two are [sic] four."

31

The World's Writing Systems

Different people find different answers to the same problems. Therefore it is not surprising that different types of writing are used by different languages and cultures. The main types are described here.

Alphabetical Each letter represents a single sound of the language. (However, a single letter can have several different pronunciations.) There are many alphabets. The Roman alphabet used by English, the Arabic alphabet, and the Greek alphabet are some examples. Can you think of any others?

Syllabic The symbols represent syllables (combinations of vowel and consonant sounds) rather than individual sounds. Japanese uses two syllabaries along with the Chinese character system.

Character The symbols represent whole words or are combined to represent words. Chinese and Japanese both use character writing. The Chinese system is the only character system surviving in the world today.

Although we can say that there are these three major types, individual languages can mix these to develop their own unique writing systems. For example, Japanese uses a system of characters along with two syllabaries and the Latin alphabet.

In addition, linguists have devised a "phonetic" system in which there are separate symbols for each sound. You can see examples of this "phonetic" system in most dictionaries. Its function is to show how words are pronounced.

我失驕楊君失柳，楊柳輕颺直上重霄九。問訊吳剛何所有，吳

ΑΒΓΔΕΖΗΘΟ◇□☐ΙΚΛΜΝΞ

Printing

CHAPTER FIVE

Practice with Printing

To print correctly, you must learn to use the space between words to show where each word stops. The space between each word is about the size of a small **o** or **a**. The space between sentences (after the period) is larger—about the size of a capital letter.

You might also notice that two circular letters are placed a little closer to each other than are two vertical letters:

pool   not   p o o l

fall   not   f a l l

This is to keep from crowding the letters—or from having too much space between the letters of a word.

A. Copying Practice

These drills are mechanical exercises to help you practice printing. Do these as quickly as you can. You must check for

- correct form of letters
- correct placement on lines
- correct spacing within words
- correct spacing between words
- correct spacing between sentences

1. Copy each of these words five times.

```
see
meat
hit
six
ship
```

age
pay
wet
head
said
sat
pull
wood
food
you
go
stop
toe
call
law
ride
eye
how
house
toy
boil
awake
asleep

2. Copy each of these words three times.

calculus

physics

wheel

quantum

computer

kilovar

plethora

oncology

zymurgy

arboretum

deductive

aeronautics

engineering

chemistry

economics

mathematics

university

xylography

juxtaposition

verisimilitude

B. Names

When printing names, remember that in English we capitalize the first letter of each part of a name. Write the names of these famous U.S. scientists twice.

Benjamin Franklin

Thomas Edison

Enrico Fermi

Rosalyn S. Yalow

James W. Cronin

C. Word Groups

Here we will focus on printing words in groups.

1. Copy this list of the first ten winners of the Nobel Prize for Physics, dividing them by country.

   Wilhelm C. Roentgen, Germany, 1901
   Hendrik A. Lorentz, Holland, 1902
   Pieter Zeeman, Holland, 1902
   Pierre Curie, France, 1903
   Marie Curie, France and Poland, 1903
   Antoine Henri Becquerel, France, 1903
   John W. Strutt, Britain, 1904
   Philipp E. A. von Lenard, Germany, 1905
   Joseph J. Thompson, Britain, 1906
   Albert A. Michelson, U.S., 1907

Britain:

France:

Germany:

Holland: _____

Poland: _____

United States: _____

2. First copy this list of 8 famous U.S. universities. Then alphabetize the list in the spaces provided.

Yale University
Harvard University
Princeton University
Brown University
Duke University
Massachusetts Institute of Technology
Columbia University
Stanford University

E. Shopping Lists

Bookstores at U.S. colleges and universities usually carry many things in addition to books. Copy this bookstore shopping list in the space provided. Divide the things on the list into "personal needs" and "school supplies." Write the words in the space given below. If needed, use two lines for an item.

```
2 ballpoint pens
toothpaste
lined 3 x 5 cards (index cards)
stamps
4 C batteries (for tape recorder)
package of file folders
```

postcards
erasable typing paper – 100 sheets
1 box paper clips
shampoo
chewing gum

School Supplies

Personal Needs

F. Poetry

Copy this poem. Use capital letters at the beginning of each line. Be sure to make all letters the same size and keep the spaces the same between words.

from "Afternoon in February"
 by Henry Wadsworth Longfellow

The day is ending,
The night is descending;
The marsh is frozen,
The river is dead.

Shadows are trailing,
My heart is bewailing
And tolling within
Like a funeral bell.

G. Quotations

Practice printing the quotations given below. Make sure your letter size and spacing between words and sentences is uniform.

1. "It is said an Eastern monarch once charged his wise men to invent him a sentence to be ever in view, and which should be true and appropriate in all times and situations. They presented him the words: 'And this, too, shall pass away.' How much it expresses! How chastening in the hour of pride! How consoling in the depths of affliction!"

    Abraham Lincoln

Notice the punctuation used for writing a quotation within another quotation. Who was Abraham Lincoln? What was his role in American history?

2. "When power leads man toward arrogance, poetry reminds him of his limitations. When power narrows the areas of man's concern, poetry reminds him of the richness and diversity of his existence. When power corrupts, poetry cleanses, for art establishes the basic human truths which must serve as the touchstone of our judgment."

John F. Kennedy

Who was John Kennedy? Why is he remembered in the U.S. (and the world)?

H. Printing Evaluation

Stop at this point and evaluate the printing exercises you have just completed.

- Do the letters have the correct shapes?
- Do the letters have the correct sizes?
- Is the spacing correct, so that you can tell where each word ends?
- Is the punctuation written in the correct manner?
- Is the punctuation at the correct place in the space or on the line?
- Do the quotations look legible and neat?

Alphabetical Writing Systems

The major alphabetical systems in the world are Roman (or Latin), Arabic, Cyrillic, and Indic.

Languages that use the Roman alphabet include English, French, German, Italian, Spanish, Turkish, Vietnamese, Fijian, Nauru, Samoan, and others.

In addition to the Arabic language, Arabic script is also used by Malaysian, Afghan, and Farsi.

Cyrillic is used for writing the Russian language and for most of the languages written in the U.S.S.R.—including Mongolian.

For all of their apparent differences, most of the languages written in India and Southeast Asia use alphabetical systems that are based on the following principles: no distinctions between capitals and lower case letters, symbols for both vowels and consonants, and written left to right on a horizontal line. Because these systems uses basic symbols that are consonant plus a vowel (with additional marks that can be used to show changes in vowels) some scholars call them "syllabic." Other scholars call them "alphabetical" because the majority of the symbols can be separated into individual consonants and vowels.

ΑΡΓΟΝΑΥΤΙΚΑ

Ἀρχόμενος σέο, Φοῖβε, παλαιγενέων κλέα φωτῶν μνήσομαι, οἵ Πόντοιο κατὰ στόμα καὶ διὰ πέτρας Κυανέας βασιλῆος ἐφημοσύνῃ Πελίαο χρύσειον μετὰ κῶας ἐύξυγον ἤλασαν Ἀργώ.

■■■■

Printing

CHAPTER SIX

Printing in Actual Use

In this chapter you will practice using printing in contexts where Americans really do use that writing style. Or at least, contexts in which they are asked "Please print" or in which they *should* print to assure clear communication. One of the problems with filling out forms is that they frequently do not give you enough space to write, so you must learn to adjust the size of your printing to fit the given space. However, when you have enough space you should print at the normal size. Stop and evaluate your writing after you have completed each exercise. Use the evaluation list given on page 44.

A. Airline Labels

Here is one of the labels airlines use to identify our luggage. Print your name and address using both capital and lower case letters. What languages are used on these tags in addition to English? Do you know why so many of these words are very similar (or the same) in these languages?

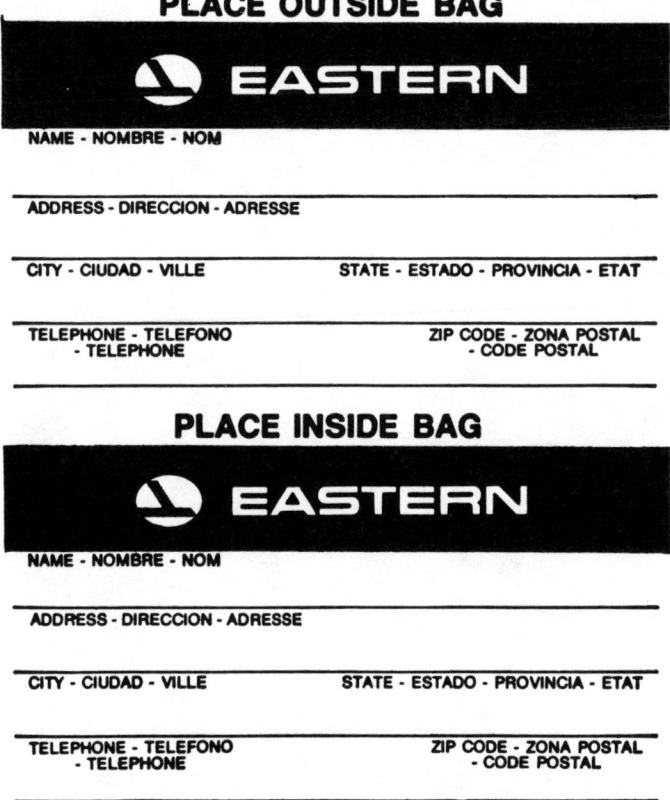

B. Answer Sheets

Here is an answer sheet for a machine-scored test. Forms similar to this one are used all over the United States. Print your name, last name first, in the blocks. Leave a space between each part of your name. Then blacken the space under each letter that corresponds to the letter. First look over the example and then fill in the blank form.

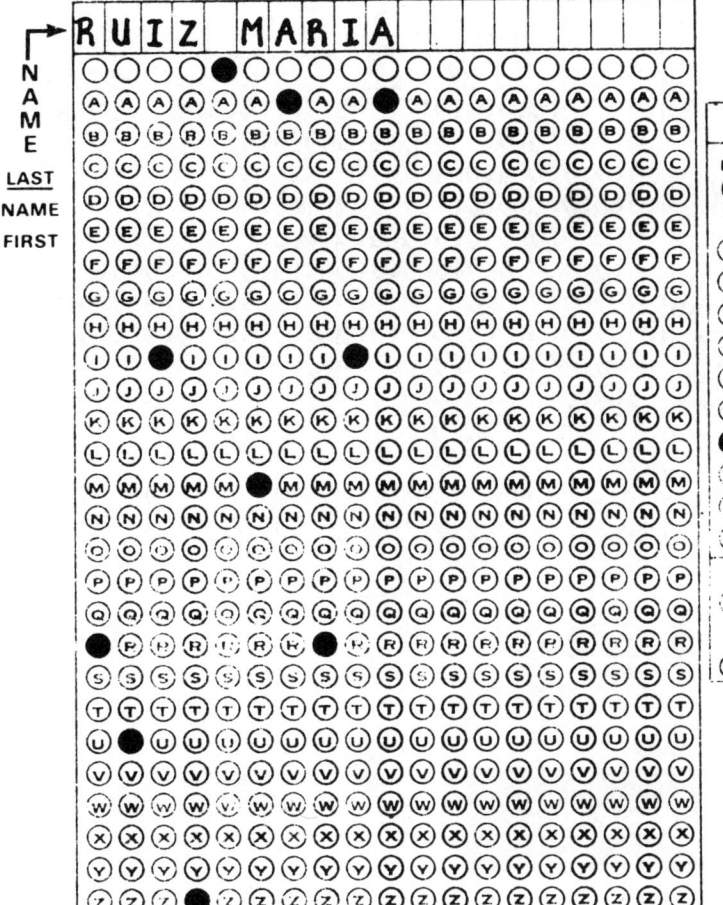

Answer Sheet

For this exercise, your identification number is 241-63-8888.

C. Application Forms

1. The TOEFL (Teachers of English as a Foreign Language) Application Form is part of the application form used by ETS for the International Testing Program and for the Special Center Testing Program. For this exercise the test center is Los Angeles, California, USA.

    This form is not for use in application for TOEFL. If you need information about TOEFL, write to

    TOEFL
    Educational Testing Service
    Princeton, New Jersey USA 08541

Sample

1983-84 TOEFL APPLICATION FORM **1** US/Canada	INTERNATIONAL TESTING PROGRAM	SPECIAL CENTER TESTING PROGRAM	ETS USE ONLY
	Test Fee .... US$21 ☐ 1	Test Fee .... US$29 ☐ 5	Fee Voucher ☐
	Test Fee + Sample Test .... US$24 ☒ 2	Test Fee + Sample Test .... US$32 ☐ 6	Sponsor Code _____
	Test Fee + Test Kit .... US$32 ☐ 3	Test Fee + Test Kit .... US$40 ☐ 7	Fee Amt. _____
	Test Fee + Test Kit + Sample Test .. US$35 ☐ 4	Test Fee + Test Kit + Sample Test .. US$43 ☐ 8	9 ☐

YOUR APPLICATION NUMBER: **D069393**

Check the appropriate box to show the amount you are enclosing.

SECTION A

1. NAME — Print your family NAME (surname), first name, then middle name. Leave a blank box between names.

`GONZALEZ JUAN`

2. STREET ADDRESS — Print your NUMBER and STREET ADDRESS. Leave a blank box after each complete number or word.

`3471 NW 18 STREET`

CITY `ANYTOWN` **STATE/PROVINCE Abbreviation** `CA` **ZIP or POSTAL CODE** `90000`

COUNTRY (not necessary for US applicants)

3. TEST CENTER

Los Angeles (CITY) California (STATE/PROVINCE) USA (COUNTRY)

3a. INTERNATIONAL TESTING PROGRAM CENTER NUMBER:
- FIRST CHOICE: `X334`
- SECOND CHOICE: `X324`

3b. SPECIAL CENTER TESTING PROGRAM CENTER NUMBER:
- FIRST CHOICE:
- SECOND CHOICE:

5. The current testing year is July 1, 1983, to June 30, 1984. Mark here how many times you have taken TOEFL during this time. Do **not** include the test date for which you are now applying.

- 0 ☒ None
- 1 ☐ Once
- 2 ☐ Twice
- 3 ☐ More than twice

TOEFL Application Form

Plan to take the TOEFL in Gainesville, Florida. Your International Testing Program choices are:

    X608 Santa Fe Community College
    X610 University of Florida

1983-84 TOEFL APPLICATION FORM 1 US/Canada	INTERNATIONAL TESTING PROGRAM	SPECIAL CENTER TESTING PROGRAM	ETS USE ONLY
	Test Fee .... US$21 ☐ 1	Test Fee .... US$29 ☐ 5	Fee Voucher ☐
	Test Fee + Sample Test .... US$24 ☐ 2	Test Fee + Sample Test .... US$32 ☐ 6	Sponsor Code _____
	Test Fee + Test Kit .... US$32 ☐ 3	Test Fee + Test Kit .... US$40 ☐ 7	Fee Amt. _____
	Test Fee + Test Kit + Sample Test .. US$35 ☐ 4	Test Fee + Test Kit + Sample Test .. US$43 ☐ 8	9 ☐

YOUR APPLICATION NUMBER: C 930722

Check the appropriate box to show the amount you are enclosing.

SECTION A

1. NAME — Print your family NAME (surname), first name, then middle name. Leave a blank box between names.

2. STREET ADDRESS — Print your NUMBER and STREET ADDRESS. Leave a blank box after each complete number or word.

CITY / STATE/PROVINCE Abbreviation / ZIP or POSTAL CODE

COUNTRY (not necessary for US applicants)

3. TEST CENTER
   CITY   STATE/PROVINCE   COUNTRY

3a. INTERNATIONAL TESTING PROGRAM CENTER NUMBER:
  FIRST CHOICE
  SECOND CHOICE

3b. SPECIAL CENTER TESTING PROGRAM CENTER NUMBER:
  FIRST CHOICE
  SECOND CHOICE

5. The current testing year is July 1, 1983, to June 30, 1984. Mark here how many times you have taken TOEFL during this time. Do **not** include the test date for which you are now applying.

  0 ☐ None   1 ☐ Once   2 ☐ Twice   3 ☐ More than twice

Michigan Test Identification Form

CONTINENTAL UNIVERSITY ENGLISH LANGUAGE ASSESSMENT BATTERY
IDENTIFICATION FORM

This identification form is required of all persons sitting for the Language Assessment Battery. Applicants must complete this form and bring it, accompanied by two (2) photos, and official identification, with them to the test. Official identification MUST be a Passport, Alien Registration Card, or National Identity Card with photo. One additional piece of identification should also be presented.

Please type or print your full name <u>exactly</u> as it appears on your official identification.

NAME _____
    (Last, or family)   (First)   (Middle)

FULL ADDRESS _____

                _____

                _____

TELEPHONE NUMBER ( )_____

Fill in number on official identification presented at time of test:

_____ PASSPORT NUMBER

_____ ALIEN REGISTRATION CARD NO.

_____ NATIONAL IDENTITY CARD NO.

Identification issued by (country) _____

BIRTH DATE _____
          (Month)   (Day)   (Year)

FATHER'S NAME _____

MOTHER'S NAME _____

NATIVE LANGUAGE _____

PLACE OF BIRTH _____

SIGNATURE _____

```
2 PHOTOGRAPHS

Attach two (2) recent
photos here. The
photos MUST look like
you do now.
```

One score report will be sent to you at the above address. You may authorize two additional score reports at no extra charge. In the spaces below, write the names and addresses of institutions to which scores should be sent.

_____   _____

_____   _____

_____   _____

_____   _____

Additional score reports cost U.S. $3.00 each. If you wish to have more score reports, print the names and addresses of additional institutions on the back of this form. YOU MUST WAIT AT LEAST SIX (6) WEEKS BEFORE TAKING THE BATTERY AGAIN, AND YOU MAY TAKE THIS TEST ONLY THREE (3) TIMES WITHING A TWELVE MONTH PERIOD. ELI'S RECORDS INDICATE THAT STUDENTS' TEST SCORES DO NOT SHOW SIGNIFICANT CHANGES IF THEY RE-TEST TOO FREQUENTLY. ELI RECOMMENDS THAT STUDENTS WAIT AT LEAST THREE MONTHS AND ACTIVELY STUDY ENGLISH BEFORE BEING RE-TESTED.

2. Here is a college application form. Practice answering these questions which are typical of application forms for U.S. colleges and universities. If you do not have a Social Security Number, use 999-99-9999.

Continental University
Continental California

Dear Student:

    We are pleased that you are interested in attending our university. Before we can consider your application, we need all of the information requested on the attached forms along with a $20 non-refundable application fee. If you have not yet taken the TOEFL, please send all other application information and the fee immediately so that we can start the application process. Please forward the TOEFL score to us as soon as it is available.

    If you have any questions, we will be happy to answer them.

General Information Sheet

CONTINENTAL UNIVERSITY
APPLICATION FOR ADMISSION

Please check one:
- ☐ New Applicant
- ☐ Previously applied but never enrolled
- ☐ Previously enrolled

PLEASE TYPE OR PRINT WITH PEN — INCOMPLETE FORMS WILL BE RETURNED WITHOUT PROCESSING

GENERAL INFORMATION (Section A)

| Last Name | First Name | Middle Name | Social Security Number |

Street Address | Area Code Day Phone Number

City | State | Zip | Area Code Evening Phone Number

Person to notify in case of an emergency (include address if different from above) | Area Code Phone Number

The following information is requested for statistical purposes and to report in compliance with State and Federal Regulations.

PERSONAL INFORMATION (Section B)

DATE OF BIRTH: _____ Month Day Year   PLACE OF BIRTH: _____ City State

PLACE APPROPRIATE NUMBER IN THE BOX FOR EACH QUESTION

- SEX: ① Male ② Female
- CITIZENSHIP: ① U.S.A.   ④ FOREIGN STUDENT VISA
  ③ RESIDENT ALIEN   ② OTHER VISA (please list) _____
- IF OTHER THAN U.S.A., CITIZEN OF: (Country) _____
- PRIMARY LANGUAGE: ① English ② Spanish ③ Other (please list) _____

In order to provide services to disabled students, the College is asking for "VOLUNTARY" self-identification of students with a specific disability. This information will be confidential and will be used for the sole purpose of aiding you to achieve your fullest potential.

PLEASE PLACE APPROPRIATE NUMBER IN BOX FOR ANY OF THE FOLLOWING DISABILITIES THAT APPLY TO YOU:
- ⓪ Not applicable   ③ Mobility Impairment   ⑥ Epilepsy
- ① Visual Impairment   ④ Cardiovascular Disorders   ⑦ Dyslexia
- ② Hearing Impairment   ⑤ Diabetes   ⑧ Other or multiple disabilities

ENROLLMENT PLANS (Section C)

TYPE OF ADMISSION:
- ① High School Graduate or Equivalency Diploma
- ② Transfer Student

PLEASE INDICATE TERM YOU WISH TO BEGIN YOUR ENROLLMENT:
- ⑧ Fall (August-December) ① Spring (January-April) ⑤ Summer (May-June) ⑥ Summer (June-August)

PREVIOUS EDUCATION (Section D)

THE LAST COLLEGE ATTENDED WAS:
- ① in the State of Florida ② out of the State of Florida ③ not applicable

HIGHEST DEGREE EARNED:
- ① None ② Associate ③ Bachelor ④ Master ⑤ Doctorate ⑥ Professional

APPLICATION AGREEMENT

I hereby apply for admission to Continental University and certify that the above information is accurate and complete to the best of my knowledge. If admitted to Continental University, I agree to abide by all the regulations of the university. I also understand that in order to take courses for credit or to receive credit for courses completed, a copy of my high school transcript is required along with official transcripts from all colleges previously attended.

Signature _____   Date _____

Education History Form

EDUCATIONAL BACKGROUND*

1 CALENDAR YEAR 19___ TO 19___	2 YOUR AGE	3 YEAR IN SCHOOL	4 GRADE STANDARD	5 KIND OF SCHOOL (ELEMENTARY, COLEGIO, ETC.)	6 FULL NAME OF SCHOOL	7 SCHOOL ADDRESS (CITY AND COUNTRY)	8 LANGUAGE OF INSTRUCTION	9 CERTIFICATES, DIPLOMAS, DEGREES, GRADUATIONS
		1						
		2						
		3						
		4						
		5						
		6						
		7						
		8						
		9						
		10						
		11						
		12						
		13						
		14						
		15						
		16						
		17						
		18						

INSTRUCTIONS

Column 1 — On each line write the appropriate years for every school year you attended.

Column 2 — Write your age. If you were 6 years old when you attended school for the first time write 6 on the first line. Continue by writing your correct age for each grade you attended.

Column 3 — These are actual years you attended school. Your first year is number 1, your second year number 2, etc. You must account for every year. If you were out of school for a length of time it must be noted. Allow one line for each year.

Column 4 — For each school year enter the standard grade, form, class, sixieme, cinquime, sexta, or whatever may be the name of the class or level you attended that year.

Column 5 — Write the kind of school you attended such as Kindergarten, Elementary, Grundschule, Volkschule, Mittelschule, Gymnasium, Lycee, Colegio, Ecole Superieur, Secondary School, Grammar School, Teacher's College, University, etc.

Column 6 — Enter the name of each school attended.

Column 7 — Write the city, village or town where each school you have attended is located. Show country if other than country of citizenship.

Column 8 — Write the language used in class by your teachers.

Column 9 — Write the name of any examination(s) you passed or certificate(s) you obtained at the end of that school year. For example, if you completed high school at the end of your twelfth year in school, on that line write: GCE, Reifezeugnis, Artium, Studentereksamen, Bachilerato, Baccalaureat, etc. (Certified translations into English of supporting documents from the secondary level and above must accompany this form.)

*Applicants must complete columns 1 through 9 — in full — to be considered for admission.

D. Add/Drop Forms

Ali Al-Qutani registered for his spring semester courses at the end of the fall semester, but he changed his plans about 2 courses. Now he wants to drop JOU 4300—Magazine and Feature Writing and ENL 4273—20th Century British Literature and to add JOU 4311—Advanced Magazine Writing and COP 3110—Introduction to Computer Programing. Fill in the form on the opposite page. Print the information requested.

    Ali's Social Security Number is 414-55-9999.

    The section numbers are   JOU 4300 1889X
                                     ENL 4273 1335X
                                     JOU 4311 1892X
                                     COP 3110 0791X.

    Ali is a 4th year student majoring in journalism so his class/college designation is 4JM. He is registering for the spring semester of this year.

E. Memos

1. You made an appointment with one of your professors, Dr. Tucker, to talk about a required paper. You have found out that your parents will be telephoning you from your country at the time of the appointment. Since it would be difficult for them to reschedule the international telephone call, you need to change the appointment. The professor is not in his office. His secretary suggests that you write him a note. Print the note here.

Departmental Memo Form

Date: _____

To: _____

From: _____

Re: _____

_____

_____

_____

_____

_____

_____

_____

_____

_____

Add/Drop Form

2. Maria Alvarez has a job on campus working in the Math Department doing clerical chores, such as answering the telephone. She had this phone conversation on the morning of January 18 at 10:40:

(Phone rings.)
Maria: "Math Department."
Voice: "I would like to speak to Dr. Zorilo."
Maria: "I'm sorry, but Dr. Zorilo is not here. Can I give him a message?"
Voice: "Tell him Bill Smith called from the Graduate School. I have to talk with him before he goes to the committee meeting this afternoon."
Maria: "Does he have your phone number, Dean Smith?"
Voice: "He should, but in case he doesn't, it is 392-5000."
Maria: "I'll put the message in his mailbox right now."
Voice: Thank you very much. Good-bye.
Maria writes the message for Dr. Zorilo.

Fill in this standard telephone message form. Print clearly.

```
To_____
Date_____ Time_____

        WHILE YOU WERE OUT
M_____
of_____
Phone_____
      Area Code   Number    Extension
  TELEPHONED         PLEASE CALL
  CALLED TO SEE YOU  WILL CALL AGAIN
  WANTS TO SEE YOU   URGENT
         RETURNED YOUR CALL

Message_____
_____
_____
_____
_____
_____
                    Operator
```

F. Labels

You are a laboratory assistant in the Botany Department. You are assigned to prepare labels for a display of wildflowers. The professor in charge tells you to print the labels using all capital letters for the common names and using all lower case letters for the Latin names. The Latin names are to be placed directly beneath the common names. Center the names on the labels.

Here is an example the professor left for you.

Example: Common name: WOOD SORREL
Latin name: oxalis montana

```
WOOD SORREL
oxalis montana
```

Make labels for these 5 wildflowers.

1. Common name: ATAMASCO LILY
   Latin name: zephyranthes atamasco

2. Common name: WINGED SUMAC
   Latin name: rhus copallina

3. Common name: BUTTERFLY WEED
   Latin name: asclepias tuberosa

4. Common name: YARROW
   Latin name: achillea millefolium

5. Common name: SHEPHERD'S NEEDLE
   Latin name: bidens pilosa

Why do these wildflowers have two names—English and Latin? Who names them?

G. Medical Forms

Most U.S. colleges and universities have inexpensive medical services for their students at an on-campus "infirmary" or clinic. For medical treatment, you will be required to fill out a medical history form similar to the one on the next page. Print the required information on this Continental University form.

Infirmary Form

CONTINENTAL UNIVERSITY
STUDENT HEALTH SERVICE

For admission to the University on _____ 198___ to 8___

1. Please type or print
2. Forward to Student Health Service three weeks prior to registration.
3. Statement provides basis for medical care while at the University, you will not be denied admission for medical reasons unless you have a condition which may be harmful to other members of the University community.

PERSONAL INFORMATION

Last Name			First Name	Middle Name	
Social Security Number	Nationality	Height	Weight	Permanent Address	
				Street	
Birthdate	Race	Age	Sex		
				City State Zip	

NEXT OF KIN OR PERSON TO BE NOTIFIED IN EMERGENCY

Name	Address
	Street
Relationship Telephone Number	City State Zip

REQUIRED MEDICAL PROCEDURES

Tuberculosis skin test within one (1) year	Date	Result	Diphtheria Tetanus Immunization within ten (10) years	Year
Rubella Titer	Date	Result	Polio series completed	Year
Or Rubella Vaccine or MMR	Date			

MEDICAL INFORMATION - DO YOU HAVE?

Allergies or sensitivities to medications	Yes	No	Any limitations on physical activities	Yes	No
Medical conditions or long term medications which may require follow up care at the University	Yes	No	Nervous or emotional problems	Yes	No
Any history of allergy, asthma, hay fever, heart disease, diabetes, etc.	Yes	No	Health Insurance	Yes	No

Elaborate on "Yes" answers. Attach statement from your physician if necessary to clarify the problem. Use the next page.

HEALTH INSURANCE INFORMATION

It is considered essential that every student be covered by some form of comprehensive health insurance. If you are now covered, state carrier or insurance company and contract number.

_____
_____
_____
_____
_____

Signature of Student   Date Signed

REQUIRED AUTHORIZATION FOR CASE OF MINOR STUDENTS: I concur in the above and authorize medical and surgical care, including examinations, treatments, immunizations, and the like, for my son or daughter. In the event of serious disease or injury, or need for major surgery, I understand that all reasonable efforts will be made to contact me; but that failure to make contact will not prevent emergency treatment necessary to help preserve life or health.

Signature of parent or quardian   Date Signed

Analyzing and Judging Your Writing

To improve your handwriting you must take the time to look carefully at what you have written and to judge what is good or bad about it. At the end of each exercise, you should stop and critically analyze what you are doing well and what you need to do better. Ask yourself these questions: "Are the letters correctly formed?" "Is the spacing correct?" "Does the writing sit on the lines properly?"

Look at this example of printing. What changes would you make to improve the writer's style?

For centuries, natural processes have helped to keep many lakes and rivers clean.

Now copy the example above and correct these problems.

Paper Money from Around the World

The paper money issued by a country is a good place to look for examples of the languages writing systems used in the country.

Canadian

Swiss

60

PART TWO

Cursive

Cursive

CHAPTER SEVEN 7

Capital Letters

Cursive (or script) handwriting is the style used by most educated adults in the U.S. Look at these two sentences:

Thomas Edison was an inventor.

Thomas Edison was an inventor.

What differences can you see? in letter shapes? in slant? in letter connections?

Chart for Cursive Letters

Aa Bb Cc Dd Ee
Ff Gg Hh Ii
Jj Kk Ll Mm Nn
Oo Pp Qq Rr Ss
Tt Uu Vv Ww
Xx Yy Zz

Chart of Capital Letters for Cursive

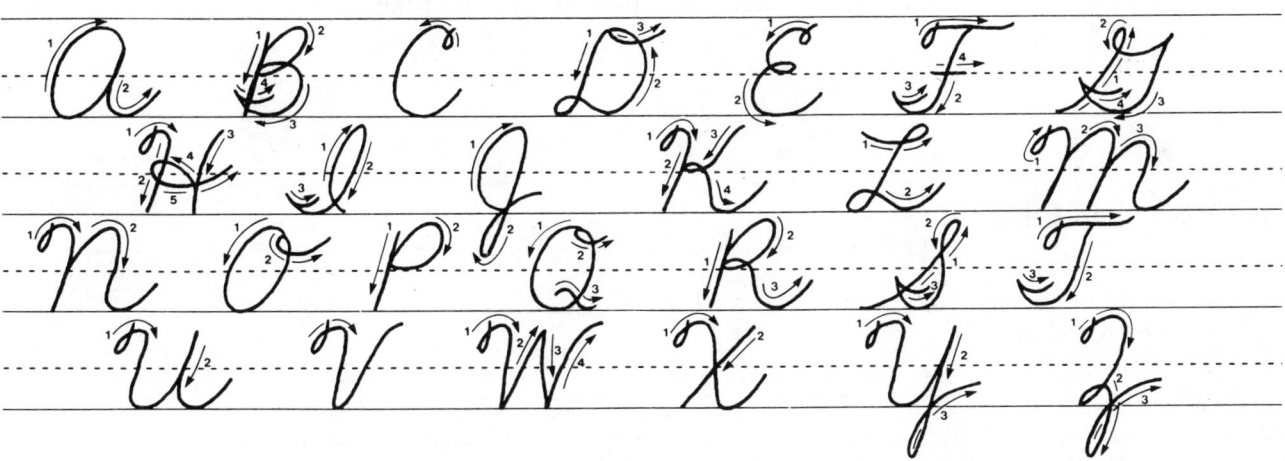

In this chapter, you will practice making capital letters in cursive. First you will work with letters that have similar shapes, then you will write them in alphabetical order.

A. Slanting Your Letters

Fill the line with letters equal in size and shape to the model. Slant your paper slightly to the left—cursive writing slants slightly to the right. The slanting is a major difference between print and cursive. Printed letters sit on straight lines drawn at a 90° angle to the writing line:

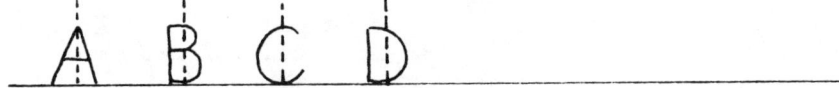

Cursive letters, however, usually slant about 30° to the right:

B. Oval Shaped Letters

All oval shaped letters start at the top and are made with one continuous stroke. Fill in the lines with the initial letter.

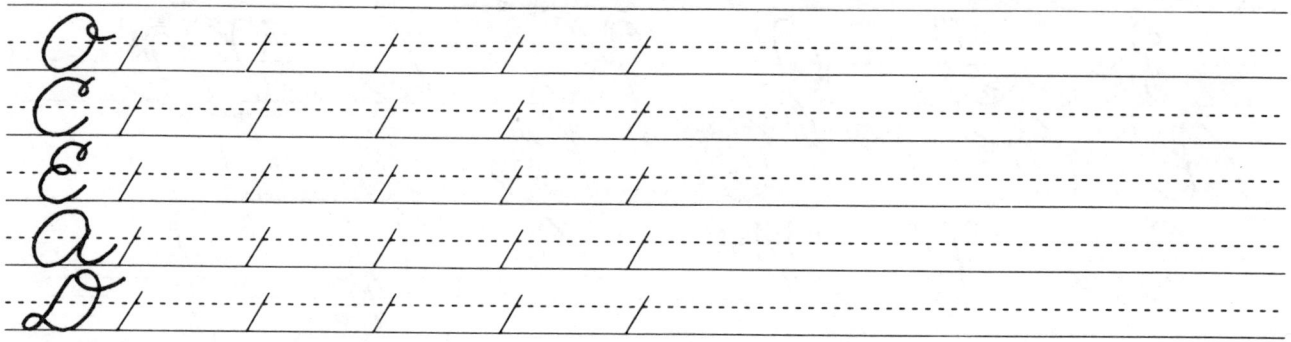

C. The Letter Q

While most people use **Q**, others use a letter that is a big version of the small cursive letter **q**. Some people use a more elaborate letter that is explained in the note on **Q** at the end of this chapter. Feel free to make your own choice. However, you need to recognize the other shapes when they are used by other writers. Fill the line with the letter.

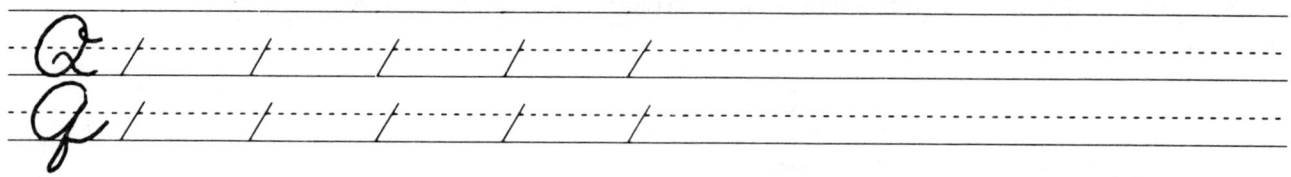

D. Letters with Loops

1. These letters all have a loop at the bottom. **B** starts at the top of the stem. Then you run the pen back up the stem to the point where the circular top begins and complete the loops. **G** and **S** start at the bottom on the left with an upward stroke.

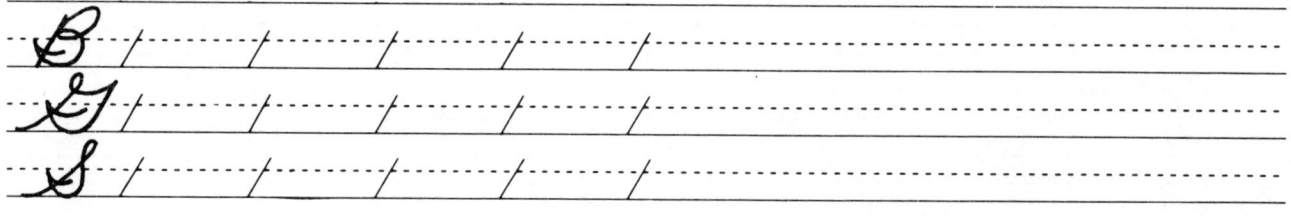

2. **T** and **F** are the same except for the bar that crosses the **F**.

3. All the letters in this group have a looped line as the first stroke. You will see many variations in the loops—both in size and shape.

   a. **H:** This letter uses two separate strokes. First you make the left side, then you lift the pen and complete the rest of the letter, starting with a down stroke.

   b. **K** and **X:** Lift your pen to make the second part of these letters.

   c. **M, N** and **W:** Notice that you do some re-tracing back up the lines. Do not lift your pen until the letter is completed.

4. These letters are similar to those of the previous group. However, the left side is rounded at the bottom to make the oval shape.

5. After making the small loop at the top, move your pen to the right and down to make the top of the **Z**. There is another small loop on the writing line followed by a descending loop below the line.

6. This letter has two loops.

7. **I** and **J** start from the line with a stroke to the left.

8. **R** is a **P** with an additional stroke at the bottom. Start both at the left top, stroke down, and then stroke back up the stem. Both letters are made with one continuous line.

E. Practice with Loops

One of the stylistic features of cursive is the use of loops at the top of many letters. When you see the writing actually used by Americans, you will notice that most people have individual variations of these loops. Some people make them much larger than the basic style. Some people do not use them at all. However, they are fundamental to the style, so you need to practice them.

1. C and E start with a stroke down and to the left and then loop back up. Fill the line with examples.

2. These letters start with a downward stroke, and use a separate stroke for the top line.

   T
   F

3. In all of these letters, the small loop is the top of a downward line.

   H
   K
   M
   N
   U
   V
   W
   X
   Y

4. With **Z**, the small loop is followed by a curving line to the right.

   Z

5. **G, O,** and **Q** all have loops, but the loops are *not* the first stroke. With **G**, start with a stroke that moves up from the line. Then make a loop at the left top of the letter.

   G

6. The loop completes the circular stroke of **O** and **Q**.

   O
   Q

F. Practicing the Alphabet

1. Write the alphabet from A to Z using all cursive capitals:

   _____
   _____
   _____

2. Now write the alphabet backwards:

   _____
   _____
   _____

Q, X, and Z

There are three cursive capital letters that most people do not use or at least, are not frequently seen in their traditional forms. Most people substitute print capitals—probably because they are easier to write and to read.

TRADITIONAL	MORE COMMON	OTHER CHOICES
2	*Q*	*q*
x	*x*	X
z	Z	

The Origin and Forms of Q

Our Roman **Q** developed from the Semitic symbol Q, which may originally have been a sign for the eye of a needle. In Roman times, the letter had two shapes: Q and Q.

Currently in the U.S., three different variations of this letter are used: Q, q, and 2.*

The last shape is not very common, but it may appear. It is still taught students in some schools.

Quickly

Quickly

Quickly

Q is combined with the letter **u** to represent the sound /kw/ as in *quick* and *quantum*. Even though the spelling in these words from French has three letters, they represent simple /k/ in *critique* or *oblique*. In words of Arabic origin, **Q** represents an Arabic pronunciation that usually comes out of an English-speaking mouth as /k/ in words like *Iraq*.

*(*Encyclopedia Britannica*, v. 18, p. 909.)

Cursive

Lower Case Letters

Combined Chart of Cursive Letters

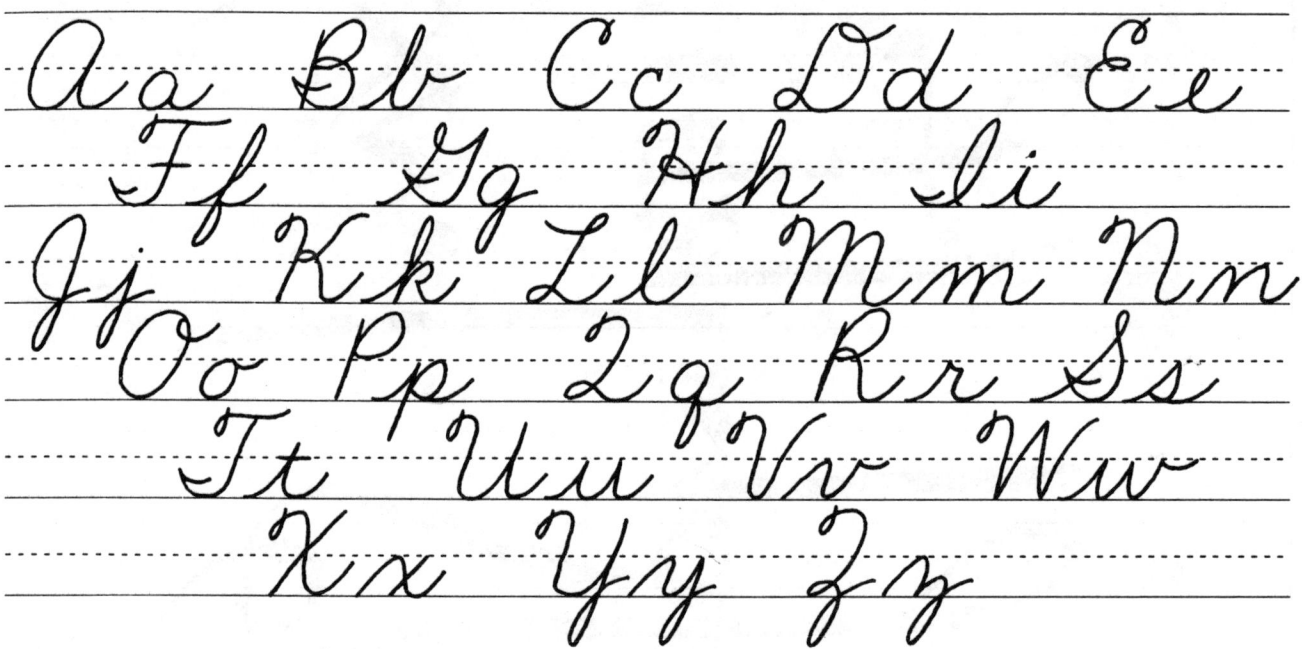

Chart for Cursive Lower Case Letters

A. Characteristics of Lower Case Letters

Fill these lines with the cursive lower case letters.

1. These letters all have an oval shape.

   o
   a
   c
   d
   g
   p
   q

2. The curve in these letters is at the bottom.

   i
   u
   w
   e

3. These curve at the top.

   n
   m
   v
   x
   y
   z

4. These two have no loops in their stems. Notice that **t** is not quite as tall as **d**.

   t

   d

5. These two have loops below the line.

   f

   j

6. All of these have tall, looped stems.

   l

   b

   f

   h

   k

7. These are unlike any of the others.

   s

   r

The Chinese Writing System

The Chinese character writing system uses symbols that represent words rather than individual sounds. Because a Chinese character represents a word and not a sound (actually many Chinese words are formed with two characters), they they may be pronounced differently by different Chinese dialects. Thus, users of the very different dialects of Northern and Southern China may have great difficulty in spoken communication, but no trouble at all in written communication. It is very similar to the difficulties encountered in our mathematical and scientific symbols which German, Russian, or French speakers may easily read while the name may be very different when spoken.

The Chinese system is usually written in vertical columns (from top to bottom) moving from right to left. Sometimes, however, it is written on a horizontal line from left to right. No spaces are left between words. Arabic numbers are sometimes used as well as the traditional Chinese number symbols.

منذ سبعة وثمانين عاما انجب آباؤنا على سطح هذه القارة أمة جديدة ولدت في ظل الحرية ووقفت ذاتها على الايمان بأن الناس جميعا خلقوا متساوين .

و اننا لنخوض الآن غمار حرب أهلية طاحنة من شأنها أن تثبت ما إذا كانت تلك الأمة ، أو أي أمة أخرى ولدت ذلك المولد و وقفت ذاتها ذلك الوقف ، قادرة على البقاء طويلا . لقد اجتمعنا على ساحة كبرى من ساحات تلك الحرب فجئنا لتكريس جانب من تلك الساحة كمثوى أخير لأولئك الذين جادوا بأرواحهم هنا حتى يتاح لتلك الأمة أن تحيا . و انه لجدير بنا و حق علينا أن نؤدي ذلك الواجب .

إلا انه ليس بوسعنا ، بمعنى أوسع ، تكريس هذه التربة أو وقفها أو تقديسها . لأن الأبطال الذين كافحوا هنا ، سواء أكانوا أحياء أم أمواتا ، قد كرسوها تكريسا لا قبل لطاقتنا الهزيلة ان تزيد فيه أو تنقص . فالعالم لن يحفل كثيرا أو يذكر طويلا ما نقوله هنا ، إلا انه لن يقوى على نسيان ما فعلوه قط . و انه لخليق بنا ، نحن الأحياء ، ان نكرس ذواتنا هنا للمهمة التي لم تنجز بعد والتي دفع بها أولئك الذين حاربوا هنا قدما حتى الآن بتلك الشهامة .

وانه لخليق بنا ان نكرس ذواتنا للمهمة العظمى التي ما زالت تواجهنا لكي نستمد من هؤلاء القتلى الكرام مزيدا من الاخلاص لتلك القضية التي بذلوا في سبيلها القدر التام الأقصى من الاخلاص ، ولكي نقرر بثقة أن هؤلاء القتلى لم يقضوا نحبهم عبثا ، ولكي تولد هذه الأمة بعون الله ولادة حرة جديدة ، ولكي لا يزول حكم الشعب للشعب من أجل الشعب عن وجه الأرض .

Cursive

CHAPTER NINE

Letter Combinations and Words in Cursive

A. Accuracy

Here are a few reminders to control the accuracy of your cursive letters.

- Remember to slant your paper to the left.
- Do not lift your pen until the end of a word—even for contractions.
- Dot **i**'s and **j**'s and cross **t**'s after the word is finished.
- Double "t" (*tt*) has one line to cross both letters.
- Spacing between letters is controlled by slant and connecting stroke.
- Keep letter size and shape consistent.
- Make sure placement of letters on the line is correct.

1. Write these words as many times as you can to fill the line.

   an
   at
   be
   me
   it
   in
   go
   do
   by
   hi

2. Write these words.

   ate
   bat

cap
dot
eat
fun
gum
hot
inn
jot
key
lie
men
not
oak
pie
rye
sat
top
use
vat
way
you

3. Write these words that have double letters in them.

pool
tool
toss

boss
ratty
moon
soon
passage
potassium
copper
sweep
occupation
effort
commence
happen
groove
channel
pattern
mass
aggregate
matter
connection
pollution
surround

4. Write these words from the Table of Chemical Elements.

actinium
barium
cadmium

dysprosium
erbium
francium
gold
helium
indium
krypton
lutetium
maganese
neodymium
oxygen
phosphorous
radium
silicon
titanium
uranium
vanadium
xenon

Do you know the symbols for these elements?

5. Write the alphabet from a to z using lower case cursive letters. Connect each letter to the following letter. Do not lift your pen until you finish the **z**. Then add the dots for **i** and **j**. Next, cross the **t**. Finally, cross the **x**.

B. Difficult letter combinations

When American students are learning to write in the cursive style, there are some combinations of letters that they find difficult to make. Try these for yourself.

1. **b** combinations

   ba
   be
   bi
   bo
   bu
   br
   by
   back
   been
   book
   bunk
   brain
   goodbye

2. **o** combinations

   oa
   oe
   oi
   oo
   ou
   ob
   oc
   od

of
on
or
os
ot
ow
coat
toe
soil
pool
through
object
lock
pod
ton
opinion
door
toss
pot
throw

3. v combinations

va
ve
vi
vo
vu

vacation
view
love
voice
revue

4. **w** combinations

wa
we
wi
wo
wu
wh
wr
ws
wave
were
wile
woe
wurst
where
wrote
knows

C. Combinations

Now combine capital letters with lower case letters in cursive. Some capital letters are seldom connected to the following lower case letters: **D L O P Q V W X F T**. In fact, connecting the capital letters is not required at all, although many people do make the connections.

1. Try writing these words with the capital connected to see how it can be done.

Ann
Bill
Charles
Edward
Gill
Hazel
Ivey
James
Kate
Mary
Nancy
Roy
Sarah
Ulysses
Yvonne
Zelda

2. Here are some common place names beginning with capital cursive letters that are not usually connected to the following letter. Close spacing between capital and lower case letters is used to show that these letters go together. Write the words.

Denver
Lansing
Orleans
Quebec

Vermont
Wyoming
Florida
Tennessee

Do you know which names are states? Which are cities? Do you know where these are located?

The Origin of Letters X, Y, and Z

What were the beginnings of **X, Y,** and **Z**? **X** was not used in any of the Semitic alphabets, but was developed in Greece. In the Cyrillic and in the modern Greek alphabet, **X** represents a sound something like **ch** in English.

In current English, we use **X** to represent pronunciation of sequences of two sounds, such as /ks/, /kʃ/, /ʃ/, /gʒ/, /gz/. **X** also represents the sound z as in anxiety.

/ks/: *box, mix*
/kʃ/: *obnoxious*
/ks/ or /ʃ/: *anxious*
/gʒ/: *luxurious*
/gz/: *exist*
/z/: *anxiety*

Notice, also, that the name of the letter is pronounced /eks/: *x-ray, x-axis*.

In words of Greek origin, x represents the sound /z/: *xylophone, xenophobe*.

We also see frequent use of **x**, pronounced /ks/, in commercial names of products and athletic teams: *Red Sox, Clorox, Windex, Trix, Corn Chex*.

Z originated as the Semitic ⟨ or *zayin* and was the seventh letter of the early Greek alphabet. The Latin alphabet did not have this letter until after the Roman conquest of Greece. **Z** represents two English sounds: /z/ as in *zeal* or *ooze* and /ʒ/ as in *azure*.

Y and **Z** were used by the Romans for borrowed Greek words that had sounds that were not in Latin. In modern English, **y** is used for vowel sounds in words like *happy* /i/, *symbol* /ɪ/, *my* /ɑi/, and many others. At the beginning of words it frequently has the sound /y/: *yet, yea, year, you, your,* and *yacht*.

Encyclopedia Britannica (Chicago: Encyclopedia Britannica, Inc.), v. 23, 1969, pp. 840, 858, and 937.

L. da Vinci

Joh: Sebast: Bach

J.W. Goethe

δομήνικος θεοθκο'πουλος
ε 'ποίε

Amerigo vespucci
piloto mor

diego Velasq'

[signature]

Rascald

Cursive

Practice with Cursive in Sentences

A. Sentences

Copy these sentences in cursive.

1. *Current interest in solar energy is not the first time people have been excited about its potential.*

2. *Reportedly, the first flat-plate collector appeared in 1774.*

3. It consisted of a wooden box with three layers of glass that heated to 140°F.

4. By the turn of the century, development had progressed to the point that efficiencies were about as good as they are today.

"Capturing and Storing Energy from the Sun," Charles K. Spillman, *Cutting Energy Costs: The 1980 Yearbook of Agriculture,* Pp. 330-341. Washington, D.C.: U.S. Department of Agriculture.

5. Lakes are more than just standing bodies of water.

6. They have physical and chemical characteristics which make them ideal homes for an immense variety of organisms.

7. The lake ecosystem is a community composed of interacting animals and plants and the physical and chemical environment in which they live.

8. The sun provides the energy for the entire system.

"What is a Lake?" *Clean Lakes and Us.* P. 6. Washington, D.C.: U.S. Environmental Protection Agency.

9. The most dramatic environmental feature of orbital space flight is weightlessness.

10. To live and work in a world in which there is no gravity is a totally new experience for space travelers.

11. *It is an experience characterized mostly for its novelty, but one with a broad range of important medical and behavioral consequences.*

Space Physiology and Medicine, Nicogossian, Arnauld E. and James F. Parker, Jr. Washington, D.C.: National Aeronautical and Space Administration, 1982.

B. Quotations

Copy these quotations from famous thinkers in paragraph form. Indent the first sentence.
Leave appropriate space between sentences.

There are three things which the superior man guards against. In youth — lust. When he is strong — quarrelsomeness. When he is old — covetousness.

— *Confucius*

You are young, my son, and as the years go by, time will change and even reverse many of your present opinions. Refrain therefore awhile from setting yourself up as judge of the highest matters.

— Plato

_____
_____
_____
_____

Do you know these wise men? Where did they live? When?

C. Printing and Cursive Practice

To check your ability with both printing and cursive, try filling in the lines in each column with the appropriate letter and form.

Typed form	Printed form	Cursive form
A	_____	_____
B	_____	_____
C	_____	_____
D	_____	_____
E	_____	_____
F	_____	_____
G	_____	_____
H	_____	_____
I	_____	_____
J	_____	_____
K	_____	_____
L	_____	_____
M	_____	_____
N	_____	_____
O	_____	_____
P	_____	_____
Q	_____	_____
R	_____	_____
S	_____	_____
T	_____	_____
U	_____	_____
V	_____	_____
W	_____	_____
X	_____	_____
Y	_____	_____
Z	_____	_____
a	_____	_____
b	_____	_____
c	_____	_____
d	_____	_____
e	_____	_____
f	_____	_____
g	_____	_____
h	_____	_____

i
j
k
l
m
n
o
p
q
r
s
t
u
v
w
x
y
z

D. Comparing Forms

You are planning a party for your friends and professors. You wrote this invitation in cursive but decided later that it might be clearer in print. Change it to print in the space provided. Which version do you prefer?

Dear Professor Smith,

My family and I would like for you and your wife to join us for dinner next Wednesday evening at 6:30. We would like to share some of the typical food and music of our country with you as a way of thanking you for your many kindnesses while I was doing my research.

I will come by your office tomorrow afternoon to see if

this time and date will be convenient for you.

Sincerely,

Use this space to print the invitation.

Writing and Commerce

Although we will probably never know exactly how writing was invented, the use of permanent written records for trade and agriculture started very early. It is certainly possible that the need to keep accurate measurement, storage, or financial records was the reason for the development of writing.

In the 3rd millenium B.C., the ancient Sumerians lived in the area that stretches from southern Iraq to the Gulf. Sumerian is the oldest well-known written language. We have many clay tablets upon which those people used to keep financial records. Thus, we know that almost 5,000 years ago, people had already discovered the value of permanent, written records of property and goods.

Written records are still of basic importance for accounting and other types of commercial record keeping and communication. Writing has also become important in advertising and other communication with consumers. A modern example is shown below. The backs of packages of "Mariquitas" brand plantain chips sold by the National Food Industries, Co. of Miami, Florida, has the list of ingredients in six languages: Laotian, Hindi, German, Arabic, English, French, and Spanish.

京海州连汉
北上杭大武

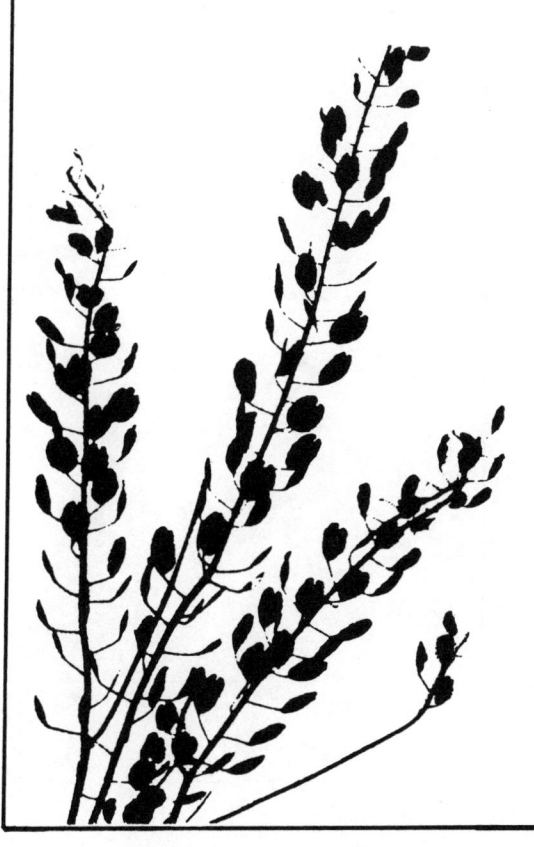

Cursive

Cursive in Actual Use

A. Blackboard Messages

In the U.S., it is common practice for messages to be left on the blackboard when a teacher cannot be present for a class. Of course, teachers also use the board to communicate when they *are* in class. Can you read these cursive samples? Match the sentences given below with the appropriate blackboard.

> Test: chapts 4-10
> class lectures
> multiple choice
> fill-in-the-blanks
> short essay

> Students of CHM 3131
> class cancelled
> today only!
> test rescheduled for
> next class meeting

1. You do not have to take the examination today.

2. The teacher is not coming to class until next week.

3. The test will have 3 parts.

4. The class has been changed to another room.

B. Writing Checks

1. Cursive is frequently used for writing checks. To pay for repairs on your bicycle, write a check to the Bike Shop for $25.90. Use today's date. Here is a model check written by a friend for school supplies:

SARAH P. GROVER	109
	4/30 19 85 5-13/11
PAY TO THE ORDER OF *Campus Book Store*	$ 25.99
Twenty-five and 99/100 ——— DOLLARS	
MEMO *supplies*	*Sarah P. Grover*
⑈011000138⑈ 32⑊4537⑊ 0109	

2. You also must pay tuition for a non-credit typing class which you are taking at the suggestion of your academic advisor. The tuition is $25.00. Make the checkced out to the *Student Union*. Use today's date.

106

3. To buy groceries last Saturday, you wrote a check for $26.62. You shopped at the Food Fare. Use last Saturday's date for this check.

D. Forms

The TOEFL application form asks you to print most information. However, in one section they require cursive to get a sample of your handwriting to use for identification.

E. Classnotes

1. You went by a friend's dorm room to borrow his classnotes from an English class you missed. He was not there. Write him a note. Tell him your problem. Ask him to telephone you at your home. Give the times you will be home. Remind him of your phone number. Use cursive.

2. Here are your friend's classnotes. (Notice that he is one of those people who prefers to print.) Copy the notes in cursive. Change his phrases into complete sentences. Change any abbreviations into full words and phrases.

```
Notes for Grammar Class            July 10
Topic: Combining sentences — relative clauses
  1. Possible to make bigger sentences
  2. Sen. 2 becomes part of Sen. 1
      1  I met the student.
      2  The student is from Holland.
      = I met the student who is from Holland.
      1  I met the student.
      2  You met the student at the party.
      = I met the student that you met
        at the party.
  3. relative clause = sentence to modify noun
```

4. relative clause is incomplete

I / met / the student.
S   V   C
  ↑ who is from Holland
    S   V   C

I / met / the student
S   V   C
         ↑ that you met at the party
           C   S   V   M

5. rel. cl. in subject

{The student who is from Holland,} speaks Dutch.
                                S   V   C

{The student that you met at the party,} speaks Dutch.
                                      S   V   C

3. Write your cursive version of the English class notes here.

109

F. Bibliography Cards

A bibliography card has all the information needed about a book or article so that other people can find the same materials. (Include the information in the bibliography of your research paper.) For example, here is a bibliography card for this penmanship textbook:

> Byrd, Patricia. Write On: A Student's Guide to Handwriting. Boston; Heinle & Heinle, 1985.

A notecard has information that you think you might use in your paper. It is usually best to have only one note on each 3 × 5 card. A notecard also has a reference to the bibliography card, so that you know where you got the information. It is good practice to put a one word key on the card to use in sorting your notes. For example:

> *Byrd WO p.   Roman numerals*
>
> *not replaced in Western Europe until 16th century*

G. Writing Bibliography Cards

In gathering notes for a research paper on scientific study of the weather, you must read the "Introduction" to *Our Physical Environment*, which starts on page 112 of this text. Make a bibliography card. Then make 4 notes. Try to rephrase the information in your own words. If you quote directly, put quotation marks around the words.

1. Write the bibliography card for the article on this 3 × 5 card:

2. Read this article. Look for information about weather forecasting in the past.

OUR PHYSICAL ENVIRONMENT
Edited by E.C. Pirkle
Part 1: The Atmosphere and Weather

Of the many factors in our physical environment that affect cultural development, few influence our living more than do the weather and climate. Every morning we waken to a day that is either rainy or sunny, cloudy or clear, warm or cold. A bright autumn day with crisp air, blue skies, and sparkling sunshine makes us feel invigorated and happy. On the other hand, a sweltering summer day may make us feel exhausted and depressed even before we start our day's work.

Our primitive ancestors undoubtedly took notice of such spectacular weather phenomena as lightning and violent storms, but they probably failed to see any patterns. Eventually people began to watch for weather signs, ascribing the phenomena to the benevolence or anger of various gods. About 700 B.C. Hesoid [sic], the Greek poet, in referring to weather and to navigation on the Mediterranean Sea, wrote:

> For fifty days after the turning of the sun . . . sailing is seasonable for men.
> Thou shalt not break thy ship, nor shall the sea destroy thy crew, save only
> if Poseidon, the Shaker of the Earth, or Zeus, the King of the Immortals, be
> wholly minded to destroy.

A few hundred years later, a few hardy souls struggled toward some rational explanation of the weather. Around 400 B.C. Hippocrates, the great physician, attempted to study the weather from a rational point of view, and about 350 B.C. Aristotle wrote his treatise *Meteorologica* that concerned weather and related phenomena. Some fifty years later, Theophrastus, Aristotle's pupil, wrote a work entitled *Book of Signs* in which were described more than 200 portents of rain, wind, and fair weather. Theophrastus even presented a few signs that were alleged to reveal the weather for the coming year. All of his proverbs and signs were related to such events as the behavior of sheep, the way a lamp burns during a storm, or the crawling of centipedes toward a wall. For the next 2,000 years this book served as a major reference work in the forecasting of weather.

Although rainfall measurements were made in India for agricultural purposes at about the same time that Aristotle lived, and wind vanes were used in Greece in about 100 B.C., it was not until the sixteenth and seventeenth centuries A.D. that real progress began. From that time on, instruments for measuring weather conditions gradually were perfected, with the result that reliable observations of weather were made and accurate records kept.

Nevertheless, progress in understanding weather was painfully slow as long as observers had no means of rapid communication over great distances. We now know that weather is global and must be considered in its entirety. Tomorrow's weather in a given location may depend on today's weather 1,000 kilometers away. After Samuel Morse developed the telegraph and sent the first public message by it in 1844, the science of meteorology advanced rapidly. Today radio, teletype, and facsimile machines for map transmission are commonly used for the dissemination of weather information.

At the present time, space and the upper atmosphere are among the fascinating new frontiers of science. These frontiers emerged after World War II. Although important speculations on the upper atmosphere were made many decades before World War II, the real impetus for such studies was the advent of rocketry. Research in this area started in earnest in 1946. Rockets with scientific payloads were launched to study the atmosphere in regions far beyond the range of aircraft and lighter-than-air balloons. A decade later, in the 1950's, the first satellites were placed in earth orbit. These satellites have shown that the upper atmosphere is truly a fascinating region for study. It is a necessary part of the total picture of the earth. These upper zones are the transitional regions between the earth and outer space. In our modern age with its complex technology, computers, and satellites, the atmosphere and weather are taking on a new and profound significance.

In the first two chapters of Part 1, a few basic scientific concepts and principles are reviewed briefly. These concepts and principles apply to all studies of the earth and its atmosphere. Chapter 3, which deals with the sun, also serves to provide background needed for a study of the atmosphere. The other chapters in Part 1 are designed to illuminate the underlying bases for atmospheric phenomena. We will explore energy balance, forces, chemical processes, large-scale air flow, and local motions of the atmosphere. We will see that weather is generated by a gigantic atmospheric machine driven by solar energy. Further, we will find that regardless of how complex our weather appears to be at any one place, the overall dynamics are guided by only a few basic laws.

3. Make your notes on these 3 × 5 cards. Remember the topic of your research paper is the historical development of weather study. Use cursive writing.

H. Postcards

While back home in your country, you decide to send postcards with local scenes to people at your university in the U.S.

1. Write a card to a professor you admire. What place in your country do you think might interest such a person? What would you tell them about the place?

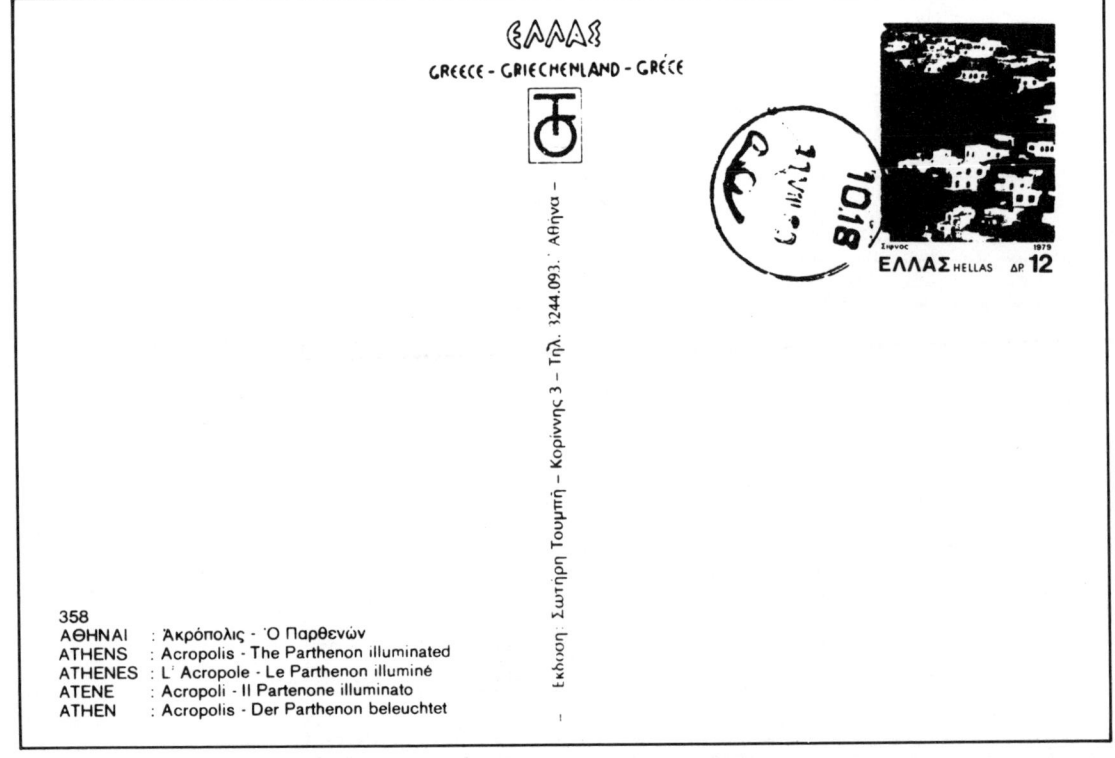

2. Write a card to a young secretary who has helped you in the departmental office. What place in your country do you think might interest such a person? What would you tell her about your vacation?

3. Send a card to a U.S. student who was very friendly and invited you to visit his home. What place might interest such a person? What could you tell him or her about that place? What might you say about your own family and your vacation?

When Should You Type?

Even if you develop an excellent style of handwriting in English, there will be times when you should type rather than write by hand. You should always type term papers and research papers. Even if the teacher gives you permission not to turn in typed papers, you put yourself at a disadvantage if you turn in handwritten papers: (1) They do not look "professional," (2) Even the best handwriting is not as consistent and clear as typing.

Other materials that should be typed include business letters, take-home examinations and any other report or paper prepared outside the classroom or laboratory.

Typing is not a difficult skill. All university students should learn to type rather than be dependent on professional typists. In some programs, students are allowed to bring typewriters to examinations. Certainly you should do so if possible.

Although there are many excellent professional typists, it is not a good rule to expect to use them to do the routine work of university study. For one thing, they need to have the manuscript from you in time to do the work. If you are doing your own typing, you can work right up to the deadline. Typing is also a good time to do final editing of the paper—checking for mistakes in your facts, grammar, and spelling—as well as style and clarity of ideas. You really cannot expect a professional typist to do all these things for you. You would have to pay a high fee if the typist also had to edit your materials.

However, there are times when you should use a professional typist. When you are ready to have your Master's thesis or Ph.D. dissertation typed, you should turn to a professional who can produce typed materials to fit the high standards required by Graduate Schools for those documents.

Cursive

Reading American Handwriting

Throughout the text we have given you samples of carefully written printing and cursive styles. In the real world, you will find that many people mix printing with cursive. Also, you will find (or probably already know) that few people write carefully and clearly all the time. This chapter is a dose of reality.

A. Handwriting Sample

Below are samples of actual handwriting from university instructors and staff members. Can you can read them? Analyze each sample by these standards:

- Does it mix print with cursive?
- Is it easy to read?
- Are the letters well formed?
- Does the spacing make each word distinct?
- Is the spacing consistent?
- Is the writing all at the same angle?
- Does the writing sit on the line evenly?

A printed version of each sample is given in the Answer Key on page **126**.

1.

Pick up texts in campus book store before first class. Class will meet in Rm. #403 Library East on M & W from 2-4.

2.

Valerie~
   Please tell
Bill that I
can't meet
him at 3 today
   ~Jen

3.

10 AM
8/8

Steve~
   Did I give you
Sections I & II of
the NUCEA
report? ~ Please
let me know ~
   Ann

4.

Your ideas are good, but the organization of the essay needs improving. Rewrite it with this in mind and also include specific examples to back up your generalities.

5.

Miss Winters,
Please send your student Roger Steele to The office at 3:30 today. Thank you.

Liz

6.

Dan,
I need some information about Busch Gardens for the Weekly. The deadline will be at 2:00 P.M. Tuesday

Thanks

Pat

7.

Kathy,
The attached invoice from Goerings indicates that you picked up the books. Please check to be sure it is correct and sign as receiving so that I can approve for payment.
Thanks
Joyce 6/15/83

8.

To: Charles Smith
Date: 4-16-83   Time: 9:30 AM

WHILE YOU WERE OUT

M/s Johnson
of P. Schumley & Associates
Phone: _____

TELEPHONED	X	PLEASE CALL	X
CALLED TO SEE YOU		WILL CALL AGAIN	
WANTS TO SEE YOU		RUSH	

Message: She needs to know the details of the proposed Special Education Tutoring Project your office sponsored.

Operator

9.

Please see me after class about making up the work you've missed; otherwise, you'll receive a failing grade.

You must get over to the writing lab immediately. You need special help on developing your compositions, especially in the area of subject/verb agreement.

Your composition lacks supporting details. You've used too many generalizations & not enough specifics.

A conclusion summarizes the preceding paragraphs; it doesn't present new information.

There will be a special TOEFL preparation session at 3:00 on Tuesday in Norman Hall 315. It's important that you be there.

10.

This composition has good ideas but you need to work on grammar form. Watch V-s ending for the present tense. Make sure every sentence has a subject.

KA

11.

Ibrahim
Enjoyed your essay. I feel you have some excellent ideas. However, you do need to work on organization of content, helping the reader (me) to understand the relationship between your ideas. See ch. 6 connectives and transitions for some vocabulary you can use to make transitions between ideas.

AC

12.

Please — I need that article you promised to let me borrow! My paper is due in two weeks, so I really need to get in gear. Give me a call at 377-0000. Thanks.

13.

The faculty meeting will be at 5:00 p.m. Friday. Mostly routine matters. Can you give us a 5-6 min. presentation/explanation of the research project you are now working on? Thanks.

Calligraphy—the Art of Writing

For most of us, handwriting has a utilitarian purpose. We write for school or for work. Artists, however, have developed beautiful writing styles that are much admired. The word for "beautiful writing," adopted from Greek, is *calligraphy*. While the Latin alphabet has inspired some beautiful writing, the greatest traditions for calligraphy are found in Arabic, Chinese, and Japanese, which incidentally, has borrowed the Chinese characters.

ANSWER KEY

Chapter One
1. AEFHIKLMNTYWXYZ
2. COS
3. BDGJPQRU

Chapter Two

A.
1. ikltvwxyz
2. cos
3. abdefghijmnpqru
4. Cc Oo Kk Vv Ww Xx Zz

B.
1. acemnorsuvwxz
2. bdfghijklpqty

Chapter Three
Roman Numerals
1. 9 = IX
2. 11 = XI
3. 19 = XIX
4. 30 = XXX
5. 300 = CCC

Chapter Six
Note on "Analyzing and Judging Your Handwriting"

Words should sit on the line.
Spacing is wrong between words.
Spacing within words needs to be improved.
These letters are not well shaped: a,p,d,r, and l.

Chapter Eleven

Blackboard #1 = B Blackboard #3 = C
Blackboard #2 = D Blackboard #4 = D

Texts for Handwriting Samples in Chapter Twelve

1. Pick up texts in campus book store before first class. Class will meet in R. 403 Library East on M & W from 2-4.

2. Valerie—Please tell Bill that I can't meet him at 3 today—Jerry

3. 10 AM 8/8 Steve—Did I give you Sections I and II of the NUCEA report?—Please let met know—JM

4. Your ideas are good, but the organization of the essay needs improving. Rewrite it with this in mind and also include specific examples to back up your generalizations.

5. Miss Winters, Please send your student Roger Steele to the office at 3:30 today. Thank you. Liz

6. Dan, I need some information about Busch Gardens for the Weekly. The deadline will be at 2:00 P.M Tuesday Thanks Pat

7. Kathy, The attached invoice from Goerings indicates that you picked up the books. Please check to be sure it is correct and sign as receiving so that I can approve for payment Thanks Joyce 6/15/83

8. To: Charles Smith
   Date: 4-16-83
   Time 9:30 AM
   Mrs. Johnson
   of P. Schumley & Associates
   Phone (914) 377-4226

   She needs to know the details of the proposed Special Education Tutoring Project your office sponsored.

9. Please see me after class about making up the work you've missed; otherwise, you'll receive a failing grade.

You must get over to the writing lab immediately. You need special help on developing your compositions, especially in the area of subject/verb agreement.

Your composition lacks supporting details. You've used too many generalizations & not enough specifics.

A conclusion summarizes the preceding paragraphs; it doesn't present new information.

There will be a special TOEFL preparation session at 3:00 on Tuesday in Norman Hall 315. It's important that you be there.

10. This composition has good ideas but you need to work on grammar form. Watch V-s ending for the present tense. Make sure every sentence has a subject. KS

11. Ibrahim Enjoyed your essay. I feel you have some excellent ideas. However, you do need to work on organization of content, helping the reader (me) to understand your ideas. See ch. 6 connectives and transitions for some vocabulary you can use to make transitions between ideas AC

12. Please—I need that article you promised to let me borrow! My paper is due in two weeks, so I really need to get in gear. Give me a call at 377-0000. Thanks.

13. The faculty meeting will be at 5:00 p.m. Friday. Mostly routine matters. Can you give us a 5-6 min. presentation/explanation of the research project you are now working on? Thanks.

Practice Sheets